HOME FREEZING
THROUGH THE YEAR

AUDREY ELLIS

HAMLYN
LONDON · NEW YORK · SYDNEY · TORONTO

Acknowledgements
The author and publishers would like to thank
the following for their co-operation in supplying
pictures for this book:
Australian Apples: page 33
Carnation Evaporated Milk: page 49
Hassy Perfection Celery: page 9
Ocean Spray Cranberries: page 60
Suttons Seeds: page 41
The illustration at the beginning of each section
drawn by Jackie Grippaudo.

Published by
The Hamlyn Publishing Group Limited
London · New York · Sydney · Toronto
Astronaut House, Feltham, Middlesex, England
© Copyright The Hamlyn Publishing Group Limited 1975

ISBN 0 600 33567 4

Filmset in England by Filmtype Services Limited,
Scarborough
Printed by Litografia A. Romero S. A.,
Santa Cruz de Tenerife, Canary Islands (Spain)
D. L. TF. 567 - 1975

INTRODUCTION

When you shop at a freezer centre it is a delight to take your choice of ready-frozen foods that are out of season. But many of these foods are available fresh in the shops during a limited period of the year at a price which makes it very advantageous to buy them and freeze them down yourself. Possibly they grow in your own garden, or a friendly farmer's field and can be yours for the trouble of picking, or a nominal charge.

This book will serve to remind you just when to look for the bargains, and more than this – suggest recipes for made-up dishes to put in store when the fresh ingredients are best and cheapest. Also, if you do grow for your freezer and eventually for your table, when to sow and what varieties will produce the best freezing results. The recipes are generally intended to serve a family of four, but can be made in larger quantities according to your needs.

Of course the circle of the seasons must be reflected in a turn-over of the freezer's contents. But it is now reckoned quite out of date to over-stock with a year's supply or more of items you will get tired of using. Who wants to eat runner beans twice every week, no matter how great the glut in the garden? You will learn with practice how much

of the precious space ought to be allocated to crops or imports that are only abundant once a year, whether to freeze whole, or reduce the basic product to something small and delicious.

When eggs are abundant and lemons cheap, I make lemon curd, and freeze it because home-made curd, delicious though it may be, forms a mould if stored in the pantry for long. It takes little freezer space, and lasts for up to a year. Use it for pies, cake fillings, spreading on brown bread and butter or as a topping for shortbread. This sort of concentrated use extends to spinach purée, sautéed mushroom slices and tomato sauce, just to name a few other examples. Spinach stores well without blanching, but think of the volume of even a couple of pounds of fresh spinach leaves!

The motto which I have evolved over years of testing, frustrating failures and exhilarating successes is this: make every square inch of freezer space pay its own way, and then see whether you can make a square centimetre do the work of an inch! Count the cost, too, season by season. By freezing what you can grow or buying at its best and cheapest, join the ever increasing number of housewives who take pride in exploiting this wonderful asset to the full.

Audrey Ellis

How to prepare vegetables for freezing

Vegetable	Preparation	Blanching time	Packing
Asparagus	Wash, trim, blanch, grade and tie in bundles.	Thin stems 2 minutes Thick stems 4 minutes	Rectangular polythene containers
Aubergines	Peel, cut into 1-inch (2·5-cm.) slices, blanch, cool and pack in layers using non-stick paper.	4 minutes	Foil trays
Beans *Broad* *French* *Runner*	Pod and blanch. Top and tail, slice or leave whole. Trim, slice thickly.	3 minutes 3 minutes 2 minutes	Polythene bags
Brussels sprouts	Peel, trim and wash. Grade, blanch, cool and drain.	3–5 minutes	Polythene bags
Carrots	Trim, peel or scrape. Wash and slice.	4 minutes	Polythene bags
Cauliflower	Trim into small sprigs, wash and blanch in salted water, drain well.	3 minutes	Polythene bags
Celery	Trim, scrub and cut into 1-inch (2·5-cm) lengths, blanch, cool, drain	3 minutes	Polythene containers
Chicory	Remove outer leaves, add lemon to blanching water, drain and pack.	2 minutes	Polythene bags
Courgettes	Wash, trim into $\frac{1}{4}$–$\frac{1}{2}$-inch ($\frac{1}{2}$–1-cm.) slices, blanch or sauté in butter.	1 minute	Polythene containers
Mushrooms	Use small button mushrooms, wash, sauté in butter for 1 minute, or slice larger ones.		Polythene containers
Onions	Peel and chop.	2 minutes	Double polythene bags
Peas *Mange tout*	Shell, blanch and cool. Trim ends, blanch and cool.	1 minute 2–3 minutes	Polythene bags Polythene bags
Peppers	Wash, remove stems, pips and pith, cut in halves or strips; blanch, drain and cool	3 minutes	Polythene containers
Spinach	Wash carefully, blanch, cool, drain well and pack	2 minutes	Polythene containers
Tomatoes	Skin, simmer for 5 minutes, rub through sieve, pack.		Polythene containers

For instructions on how to blanch vegetables see page 43.

How to prepare fruit for freezing

Fruit	Preparation	Packing
Apples	Peel, core and slice into cold salted water. Blanch 1 minute or steam blanch 2 minutes. Freeze dry in a dry sugar or syrup pack. Can be frozen as purée sweetened if liked.	Polythene bags or polythene containers
Apricots	Wash, halve and stone, syrup pack, add ascorbic acid.	Polythene containers
Blackberries	Wash only if necessary and drain then remove hulls. Freeze dry in a dry sugar or syrup pack.	Polythene containers
Blackcurrants and redcurrants	Sprigs – wash and drain, open freeze then dry sugar pack. Or top and tail, dry sugar pack.	Polythene bags or polythene containers
Cherries	Stalk, wash and drain. Open freeze then pack dry in a dry sugar or syrup pack.	Polythene bags
Damsons	Wash, halve and stone, syrup pack or as cooked purée.	Polythene containers
Gooseberries	Wash and drain, dry sugar or syrup pack.	Polythene bags or polythene containers
Grapes	Leave seedless grapes whole, or skin and pip, syrup pack.	Polythene containers
Oranges	Juice can be frozen and packed as ice cubes. Grate peel and mix with sugar. Segment or slice flesh, dry sugar or syrup pack. Freeze Seville oranges whole.	Polythene bags Polythene containers Polythene bags
Peaches	Skin, halve and stone, syrup pack with ascorbic acid. Can be frozen as purée with lemon juice and sugar.	Polythene containers
Pears	Slice, poach in boiling syrup $1\frac{1}{2}$ minutes, drain, cool and freeze with syrup or pack in cold syrup with ascorbic acid.	Polythene containers
Pineapple	Peel, core and slice. Dice or crush, layer with freezer film and sprinkle with sugar, or syrup pack.	Polythene containers
Plums	Wash, halve and stone, dry sugar or syrup pack. Can be frozen as cooked purée.	Polythene containers
Raspberries and loganberries	Wash only if necessary, drain and then hull, open freeze and pack dry, dry sugar pack or as purée.	Polythene containers
Rhubarb	Wash, trim and cut into 1-inch (2·5-cm.) lengths, blanch in boiling water 1 minute, cool, pack in syrup.	Polythene containers
Strawberries	Wash only if necessary, drain and then hull, open freeze and pack dry sugar or syrup pack. Can be frozen as purée if preferred.	Polythene containers

JANUARY

Lemon vichyssoise

2½ lb./1¼ kg. leeks
1 large onion
1 oz./25 g. butter
2 large potatoes
grated zest and juice of
  ½ lemon

2 pints/generous litre
  chicken stock
salt and pepper

Slice the leeks. Chop the onion finely and cook in
the butter over a gentle heat for about 5 minutes.
Peel the potatoes and cut into cubes and add to the
pan with the leeks, and grated zest and juice of the
lemon half. Stir well and simmer gently for a
further 8 minutes. Add the stock and seasoning
to taste; increase the heat. Cover and cook gently
for about 20 minutes. Cool slightly, then liquidise
or sieve the mixture. Cool.
To freeze Pour into polythene containers, seal
and label.
To serve Defrost at room temperature, or overnight in the refrigerator. Stir 1 tablespoon single
cream into each portion of soup and sprinkle with
chopped chives. Serve very cold. If required hot,
tip the frozen soup into a saucepan and heat very
gently. When serving, add cream and chives as
above.
Note Frozen soups taste better if cream as an
ingredient is added at the reheating stage; this
also saves storage space.

Turkey and celery casserole
(Illustrated)

1¼ lb./550 g. turkey
  breast
1½ tablespoons seasoned
  cornflour
6 sticks celery

1 onion
4 tablespoons corn oil
1 chicken stock cube
½ pint/3 dl. boiling water
1 canned pimiento

Cut the turkey into 1-inch (2·5-cm.) cubes and
coat in the seasoned cornflour. Chop the celery
and onion finely. Heat the oil in a pan or flameproof casserole and sauté the prepared vegetables
until softened, but not browned. Dissolve the
stock cube in the boiling water and add to the pan.
Cover and simmer for 20 minutes. Chop the
pimiento and add to the pan. Blend the remaining
seasoned cornflour with 1 tablespoon liquid from
the pimiento can and add to the casserole, stirring.
Continue cooking until the sauce is clear and
slightly thickened. Cool.
To freeze Pack in polythene or foil containers
(or use a foil-lined casserole; freeze until solid then
remove from the casserole, fold over the extra foil
and seal to make a neat parcel), seal and label.
To serve Reheat gently over a low heat, stirring
frequently, for about 40 minutes. Just before
serving, check the seasoning and sprinkle with
2 oz. (50 g.) grated Cheddar cheese. If liked, chopped
parsley can be added for colour contrast.

Turkey and celery casserole

Cheesy fish cakes

8 oz./225 g. steamed cod
8 oz./225 g. mashed
   potatoes
2 teaspoons chopped
   parsley
2 oz./50 g. Cheddar
   cheese, grated

1 oz./25 g. butter
salt and pepper
1 egg, beaten
breadcrumbs for coating
oil for frying

Flake the cod and mix thoroughly with the potato, parsley and cheese. Melt the butter and blend with the fish and potato mixture, together with seasoning and just enough beaten egg to bind. Divide the mixture into eight portions and form each into a round flat cake. Dip each cake into beaten egg then coat with breadcrumbs. Heat the oil and use to cook the cakes, turning once. Drain on absorbent paper and cool.
To freeze Pack with foil dividers in polythene bags or containers, seal and label.
To serve Fry from the frozen state.

Butterscotch sauce

1 oz./25 g. butter
2 oz./50 g. soft brown
   sugar
6 tablespoons golden
   syrup
1 tablespoon custard
   powder

juice of 1½ lemons
1 teaspoon grated lemon
   zest
¾ pint/4 dl. water

Melt together the butter, sugar and syrup in a saucepan. Blend the custard powder with the lemon juice and zest. Off the heat, pour the water into the syrup mixture. Stir, then pour this into the custard. Mix thoroughly and return to a gentle heat, stirring constantly, until the sauce is smooth and thickened. Cool.
To freeze Pour into small polythene containers, seal and label.
To serve Defrost in the refrigerator. This sauce is excellent as a topping for ice cream, or, if gently warmed, as an accompaniment to steamed sponge puddings.

Golden raisin roll

6 oz./175 g. plain flour
1½ teaspoons baking
   powder
½ teaspoon salt
4 oz./100 g. shredded
   suet
4 oz./100 g. stoned
   raisins or sultanas

½ pint/3 dl. milk
3 tablespoons golden
   syrup
2 oz./50 g. fresh white
   breadcrumbs

Sieve the flour, baking powder and salt into a bowl and add the suet and raisins. Stir in the milk and mix to a soft dough. Roll out into a rectangle, about 8 inches (20 cm.) by 10 inches (26 cm.) and brush the edges with water. Spread golden syrup in the centre and sprinkle the breadcrumbs over. Roll up from the shorter side into a Swiss roll shape. Grease a sheet of foil and wrap this loosely around the roll. Steam for about 2 hours. Cool.
To freeze Wrap in a second, firm layer of foil, seal and label.
To serve Remove the outer foil layer and steam for about 1 hour. Serve with syrup sauce, cream or custard.

Frosted coupes

3 oranges
2 grapefruit

6 oz./175 g. sugar
2 egg whites

Cut the oranges in half, squeeze the juice and scoop out the flesh to provide six orange cases. Grate the zest from 1 grapefruit and squeeze the juice from both. Make the fruit juices up to 1 pint (6 dl.) with water and place in a pan with grated zest and sugar. Heat slowly, stirring until the sugar has dissolved, then boil for 10 minutes. Cool and strain into a polythene bowl. Place in the freezer until mushy. Remove from the freezer, beat until grainy, then fold in the stiffly beaten egg whites. Spoon into the orange cases and turn the rest of the mixture into a rigid-based polythene container.

To freeze Open freeze the orange cases, put together in pairs with a foil divider and mould in foil. Label. Seal and label the container.

To serve Separate the filled orange halves and top with a few fresh orange segments and sugar-frosted mint leaves. Scoop the mixture from the container into sundae glasses. Store for a maximum of 6 months.

Freezing hints

This is the time of the year, when stocks are run down after the Christmas festivities, to defrost and sort out your freezer.

Make a New Year's resolution to keep a proper freezer log, writing in new additions and crossing off items immediately you take them from the freezer. Or, keep an index file with duplicate labels, one for the package of food and one for the 'memory bank'.

Cheese can be frozen in handy 1-lb (450-g.) wedges, smoothly moulded in foil. Choose from Gouda, Edam, Cheddar, Cheshire or other hard cheeses. Avoid freezing the crumbly-type cheeses such as Lancashire. Pack small quantities of grated cheese in rigid-based polythene containers or bags. You will find this invaluable for quick toppings and fillings. Cream and curd cheeses need to be beaten to restore their texture after defrosting; add a little cream to cottage cheese. Store cheeses for a maximum of 6 months (cottage cheese 3 months only).

Pack Seville oranges in bags and use them to make marmalade when convenient. All citrus fruits can be frozen as segments, or slices in a 40% sugar syrup, or sliced in sugar. Another alternative is to squeeze the juice, freeze it in ice trays and store the frozen cubes in polythene bags. Grate the zest and store it in 2-oz. (50-g.) polythene tumblers. Use for flavouring cake, scone and biscuit mixtures. (Store fruit for a maximum of 10 months; grated zest for only 3 months.)

Steamed puddings make a welcome pudding at this time of the year. If you prefer a layer pudding, roll out the dough, form it into circles to fit a greased foil basin. Arrange a dough circle in the bottom of the basin, spread over 1 tablespoon golden syrup, add another circle of dough. Continue in this way until the basin is filled to within 1 inch (2·5 cm.) of the top, ending with a layer of dough. Cover and steam for about 2 hours. Cool, then freeze. To serve, re-steam for about 1 hour.

Buys of the month

Fish Salmon, mackerel, cod, halibut, turbot, sole, mussels, scallops
Meat, poultry and game New Zealand lamb, turkey, hare, partridge, pheasant, pigeon, venison
Vegetables Brussels sprouts, celery, carrots, broccoli, leeks, parsnips, turnips, chicory, horseradish
Fruit Cooking apples, Seville and sweet oranges, grapefruit, lemons, limes, tangerines, pineapples
Miscellaneous Dates, figs, glacé fruits (The stock left over after Christmas can often be purchased cheaply and will store for up to 1 year.)

FEBRUARY

Game soup

2½ oz./65 g. butter	bouquet garni
2 small wood pigeons	3 beef stock cubes
4 oz./100 g. shin of beef	2½ pints/1¼ litres boiling
3 outer stalks celery,	water
sliced	salt and pepper to taste
1 onion, sliced	1¼ oz./35 g. flour
1 carrot, sliced	¼ pint/1½ dl. red wine

Melt half the butter in a frying pan and use to
brown the pigeons on all sides. Remove from the
pan, split each pigeon in half and place in a large
saucepan. Brown the beef in the same way and
add to the saucepan. To the butter remaining in
the pan, add the vegetables and cook until all are
browned. Place the contents of the frying pan in
the saucepan with the bouquet garni, stock cubes,
boiling water and seasoning. Bring to the boil,
cover and simmer for about 1½ hours. Strain the
soup and dice the pigeon flesh and beef. Melt the
remaining butter in a clean pan, stir in the flour
and gradually add the strained soup and the wine,
stirring. Bring to the boil, stirring constantly;
cook until slightly thickened and smooth. Stir in
the diced meat and leave to cool.

To freeze Pour into one or two polythene containers, leaving a headspace. Seal and label.

To serve Turn the frozen soup into a saucepan, add
a very little water (about 4 tablespoons) and reheat
gently to boiling point, stirring frequently. Taste
and adjust seasoning, then simmer for 5 minutes.

Rhubarb tart
(Illustrated)

2 lb./1 kg. shortcrust	1 tablespoon cornflour
pastry	3 oz./75 g. castor sugar
1 egg white	grated zest of 1 lemon
3 lb./1½ kg. early	
rhubarb	

Grease three 8-inch (20-cm.) shaped foil plates.
Roll out two-thirds of the pastry and use to line
the foil plates. Brush the pastry with lightly beaten
egg white and chill. Trim, wash and cut the
rhubarb into 1-inch (2·5-cm.) lengths. Divide the
rhubarb between the three pastry-lined plates.
Mix together the cornflour, sugar and grated zest
and sprinkle over the rhubarb. Roll out the remaining pastry and use to make three lids. Dampen the
edges, place on the lids and flake and flute the
edges. Decorate with pastry leaves made from the
trimmings of the pastry.

To freeze Cover each tart with foil. Seal and label.

To serve Uncover and cut a steam vent. Brush
the top with milk and sprinkle with sugar. Cook,
from the frozen state, in a hot oven (425°F, 220°C,
Gas Mark 7) for 30 minutes.

Rhubarb tart

Jugged hare with forcemeat balls

1 hare	1 medium onion
2 oz./50 g. dripping	salt and pepper
2 rashers bacon, chopped	bouquet garni
1½ pints/scant litre stock	1 tablespoon redcurrant
2 oz./50 g. flour	jelly

Ask the butcher to skin, paunch and joint the hare. Wipe the joints. Melt the dripping in a large pan or flameproof casserole and use to fry the hare joints until lightly browned, with the bacon. Add sufficient stock to cover the meat, then stir in the flour moistened with a little water. Slice the onion and add to the pan with the seasoning and bouquet garni. Cover and simmer, or place in a moderate oven (325°F, 160°C, Gas Mark 3) for about 3 hours, until the meat is tender. Stir in the redcurrant jelly. Cool.

To freeze Pack in a shaped foil container, cover with a lid or foil, seal and label.

To serve Defrost and reheat in a moderate oven (350°F, 180°C, Gas Mark 4) for about 1½ hours, adding the forcemeat balls – see the following recipe – 20 minutes before serving.

If liked, add 3–4 tablespoons red wine to the casserole when reheating.

Forcemeat balls

4 oz./100 g. fresh white breadcrumbs	2 oz./50 g. suet
2 teaspoons chopped parsley	grated zest of ½ lemon
	1 egg, beaten
1 teaspoon chopped thyme	seasoned flour for coating
	oil for frying

Mix all the ingredients together, binding with the beaten egg. Form into small balls and toss in seasoned flour to coat. Fry in hot oil for about 10 minutes, turning until nicely browned, and cooked through. Drain on absorbent paper and cool.

To freeze Pack in polythene bags, seal and label.

To serve Allow to defrost at room temperature for about 30 minutes. Twenty minutes before the jugged hare is ready to serve, add the forcemeat balls to the dish in which it is being reheated.

Chicory with ham

8 small heads chicory	¼ teaspoon black pepper
8 thin slices ham	¼ teaspoon grated nutmeg
¾ pint/4 dl. savoury white sauce (see method)	8 oz./225 g. Gouda cheese, grated

Cook the chicory in salted water for 10 minutes. Drain well, reserve the liquid and cool. Wrap each chicory head in a slice of ham and pack the rolls closely together in a buttered ovenproof dish, or foil container. Make the sauce, using half milk and half chicory liquid and stir in the pepper, nutmeg and cheese. Pour over the rolls. Cook in a moderately hot oven (375°F, 190°C, Gas Mark 5) for 20 minutes. Cool.

To freeze Cover, seal and label.

To serve Defrost, cover the top with 2 tablespoons toasted breadcrumbs and dot with butter. Reheat in a moderately hot oven (375°F, 190°C, Gas Mark 5) for 25 minutes. Store for a maximum of 4 months.

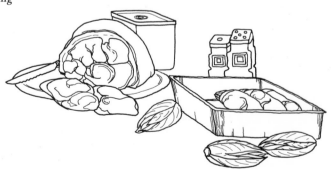

Curry-in-a-hurry

5 oz./150 g. onion
8 oz./225 g. celery
1 clove garlic
3 oz./75 g. butter or
    margarine
12 oz./350 g. cooked
    lamb, cubed

1 teaspoon salt
2 teaspoons curry
    powder
2 tablespoons plain flour
1 pint/6 dl. gravy or
    thickened stock

Slice the onion, chop the celery and crush the garlic. Heat the butter in a frying pan and use to sauté the vegetables until lightly coloured. Add the lamb, salt and curry powder. Stir in the flour until well blended, then add the gravy or stock. Cover the pan and simmer for 30 minutes. Cool.
To freeze Pack in polythene or foil containers, seal and label.
To serve Reheat gently over a low heat, stirring frequently, for about 40 minutes. Serve with boiled rice, mango chutney and sliced bananas.

Gingered kebabs

1 lb./450 g. rump steak,
    cubed
Marinade
2 teaspoons corn oil
¼ pint/1½ dl. orange juice
1 tablespoon lemon juice
3 tablespoons tomato
    ketchup

1 tablespoon demerara
    sugar
½ teaspoon ground ginger
2 teaspoons made mustard
1 teaspoon salt
To serve
8 oz./225 g. mushrooms,
    halved

Mix together all the ingredients for the marinade and place in a saucepan. Bring slowly to the boil, stirring constantly, then simmer for 3 minutes. Cool. When cold, add the meat and stir well.
To freeze Pack the meat and marinade in a polythene container, seal and label.
To serve Defrost, still sealed, in the refrigerator overnight. Thread the meat on four skewers, alternating with halved mushrooms. Brush with the marinade and grill for about 5–8 minutes, turning frequently and basting with the marinade.

Jaffa cheesecake

1 lb./450 g. cream cheese
1 oz./25 g. icing sugar
2 eggs, separated
¼ pint/1½ dl. double
    cream
1 large orange

1 envelope gelatine
2 tablespoons water
8 oz./225 g. chocolate
    digestive biscuits
4 oz./100 g. butter

Beat together the cream cheese, icing sugar, egg yolks and cream until smooth. Finely grate the zest from the orange and squeeze the juice. Add to the cheese mixture and beat again. Dissolve the gelatine in the water in a basin over a pan of simmering water. Cool and beat into the cheese mixture. When the mixture begins to thicken, fold in the stiffly beaten egg whites. Divide between two 6- or 7-inch (15- or 18-cm.) cake tins with loose bottoms and allow to set. Crush the biscuits with a rolling pin. Melt the butter in a saucepan, add the biscuit crumbs and stir well. Divide this mixture between the cheesecakes. Spread evenly and smooth the tops with a metal spoon, pressing the crumbs down gently.
To freeze Open freeze in the tins until solid. Dip the tins in hot water for 5 seconds, slide off the tins and turn each cheesecake over on to a plate or sheet of foil. Ease off the cake tin base. Return to the freezer to harden the tops, then over-wrap each plate and cheesecake with a polythene bag or foil. Seal and label.
To serve While still frozen, remove the wrapping and defrost at room temperature for about 3 hours. Decorate the top with a little grated chocolate.

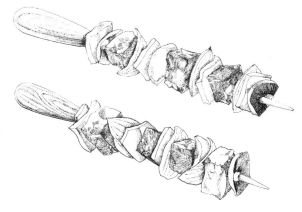

Golden grapefruit sponge

5 oz./150 g. self-raising
    flour
pinch salt
3 oz./75 g. butter
4 oz./100 g. castor sugar

2 eggs, beaten
1 tablespoon milk
grated zest of ½
    grapefruit

Sieve the flour and salt together. In a separate bowl, cream the butter and sugar until light and fluffy and gradually add the eggs, alternately with the flour. Beat in the milk and grapefruit zest. Pour the mixture into a greased foil pudding basin.
To freeze Cover with foil, seal and label.
To serve Steam the frozen pudding for about 2 hours and serve with a sauce made by liquidising canned grapefruit segments with a little sugar and evaporated milk.

Freezing hints

Look out for big, well-shaped Jerusalem artichokes – they should be at their cheapest about now. Peel them and cook until soft in strong chicken stock with a little lemon juice added. Blend in the liquidiser (or press through a sieve), cool and freeze in polythene tumblers, leaving headspace. Defrost and blend two tumblers of purée with one tumbler of milk, season and thicken to taste. Serve with croûtons. Store for a maximum of 10 months.

Double-crust pies can be made with most raw fruits – when they come into season – cherries, blackcurrants, redcurrants, gooseberries, apples and blackberries together (the pleasing pink colour masks any discolouration of the apples). Stone fruits which need to be sliced, are better frozen lightly poached in sugar syrup than uncooked. As a time-saver, line foil pie plates with pastry, freeze, together with the same number of plain pastry circles for lids. Remove the pastry cases, line the same plates with freezer film, pour in the cooked fruit and open freeze. When solid, pack the pastry cases stacked with lids, and fillings separately. To serve, peel off the freezer film, assemble the base, filling and lid in a pie plate, and bake in a hot oven (425°F, 220°C, Gas Mark 7). Store for a maximum of 4 months.

When freezing baked flan cases and tartlets they should be packed in rigid-based containers to prevent them being damaged in the freezer. Empty flan cases take about 1 hour to defrost. They may be crisped in a moderate oven (350°F, 180°C, Gas Mark 4) for about 5 minutes. Fill with a sweet or savoury filling.

Although the pre-frozen unbaked pie gives a fresher, crisper crust, it is possible to bake the pie before freezing. If you plan to do this, slightly under bake the pie as it will have further cooking during the reheating. It is important to cool the pie completely before freezing and freeze it on a flat surface so that the filling remains even. To serve, thaw at room temperature for about 30 minutes, then complete the defrosting and reheating in a moderate oven for 30 minutes.

If pineapples are plentiful, pack slices, separated by freezer film dividers, or in a 60% sugar syrup, or crushed, adding 6 oz. (175 g.) sugar to each 1 lb. (450 g.) of fruit.

Remember to exclude all unnecessary air when packing. Leave headspace for the expansion of the water content only of semi-liquid foods.

Buys of the month

Fish Salmon, mackerel, shrimps, herrings, mussels, whitebait
Meat, poultry and game New Zealand lamb, pork, chicken, capon, goose, hare, venison, partridge, pheasant, snipe, plover, teal
Vegetables Jerusalem artichokes, cabbage, spring greens, swedes, cauliflower, celeriac, Brussel tops, leeks, potatoes, chicory
Fruit Avocados, pineapple, grapes, grapefruit, rhubarb, apples, pears

MARCH

Beef and bean pot

1 lb./450 g. haricot beans	2 oz./50 g. dripping
1 beef stock cube	1 teaspoon dried mixed
4-oz./100-g. piece fat	herbs
salt bacon	salt and pepper
2 lb./1 kg. shin of beef	4 oz./100 g. fresh white
2 large onions	breadcrumbs
1 clove garlic	

Soak the beans in cold water overnight. Drain
and pour over just enough fresh water to cover.
Add the stock cube, bring to the boil and cook
for 5 minutes. Leave, covered, to stand while
preparing the other ingredients. Cut the bacon
into small dice and the beef in large dice. Chop
the onions and crush the garlic. Melt the dripping
and use to fry the bacon, beef, onion and garlic
for 3 minutes. Transfer to an ovenproof casserole
and add the beans with their cooking liquid, the
herbs and salt and pepper to taste. Cover with
the breadcrumbs and cook uncovered in a cool
oven (300°F, 150°C, Gas Mark 2) for 3 hours, until
the meat is tender. Cool.
To freeze Cover with a lid or foil, seal and label.
To serve Defrost, cover with foil and then reheat
in a moderately hot oven (375°F, 190°C, Gas Mark
5) for 30 minutes.

Vegetable curry sauce

1½ pints/scant litre water	3 large onions
8 oz./225 g. lentils	4 tablespoons corn oil
large pinch salt	3 large tomatoes, skinned
1 tablespoon curry	and sliced
powder	

Put the water into a saucepan and bring to the
boil. Add the lentils, salt and curry powder and
return to boiling point. Cover and simmer for
about 1 hour, until the lentils are tender and
mixture is very thick. Slice the onions very thinly.
Heat the oil in a frying pan and use to fry the
onions and tomatoes until softened but not
browned. Combine the mixtures and leave to
cool.
To freeze Pack in a polythene container, leaving
a headspace. Seal and label.
To serve Turn the contents into a saucepan and
reheat gently, stirring. Stir in 2 oz. (50 g.) small
raw cauliflower florets, 2 oz. (50 g.) finely sliced
raw carrot and 1 oz. (25 g.) sultanas. Stir over a
moderate heat for 3 minutes. (This recipe gives 2
servings if the dish is served as a main meal, 4 if
served as an accompaniment.)
Note Other vegetables can be added to the basic
curry sauce instead of cauliflower and carrots; try
diced swede and parsnip for a change, and shredded
coconut instead of sultanas.

Poacher's pasties

1 lb./450 g. shortcrust pastry	1 carrot
12 oz./350 g. boneless rabbit	1 teaspoon dried mixed herbs
6 oz./175 g. potatoes	3 tablespoons stock
1 medium onion	salt and pepper

Divide the pastry into eight equal pieces and roll each out into a circle. Dice the rabbit and potatoes. Chop the onion and carrot finely. Mix together the rabbit, herbs, potato, onion and carrot. Season and moisten with the stock. Divide the filling between the pastry circles and fold each one over to form a semi-circle. Dampen, seal and flute the edges.

To freeze Pack in polythene containers, seal and label.

To serve Brush the pasties with beaten egg and bake from the frozen state in a hot oven (425°F, 220°C, Gas Mark 7) for 15 minutes, then reduce the heat to moderate (350°F, 180°C, Gas Mark 4) and bake for a further 35 minutes.

Chicken en cocotte

1 medium chicken, or 4 chicken portions	2 carrots, chopped
salt and pepper to taste	4 tablespoons brandy
1 oz./25 g. butter	4 tomatoes
2 tablespoons olive oil	bouquet garni
4 oz./100 g. fat bacon, diced	½ teaspoon ground allspice
4 shallots or spring onions, chopped	½ pint/3 dl. red wine

Cut the chicken into serving pieces and season to taste. Heat the butter and oil in a flameproof casserole and use to sauté the diced bacon until brown. Remove the bacon and add the chopped shallots and carrots. Cook gently until the vegetables soften, stirring continuously. Add the chicken pieces and brown on all sides then return the bacon pieces to the casserole. Warm the brandy in a small pan or ladle, ignite and pour over the chicken. Skin and chop the tomatoes and add to the casserole with the bouquet garni, allspice and wine. Bring to the boil, cover and allow to simmer over a low heat for about 1 hour, until chicken is very tender. If the sauce reduces too quickly add more wine or a little chicken stock. Remove the bouquet garni. Cool.

To freeze Pour into a shaped foil container and cover, or freeze in the casserole. Seal and label.

To serve Place the foil container, still frozen, in a moderately hot oven (400°F, 200°C, Gas Mark 6) for about 1 hour, breaking up the contents with a fork after the first 30 minutes. If in a flameproof casserole, reheat very gently to boiling point, stirring frequently to prevent sticking, then simmer for 10 minutes.

Chicken and mushroom pie

10 oz./275 g. frozen shortcrust pastry, defrosted	1 oz./25 g. butter
	1 oz./25 g. flour
1 chicken stock cube	6 oz./175 g. cooked chicken, diced
¼ pint/1½ dl. boiling water	4 oz./100 g. canned button mushrooms
¼ pint/1½ dl. milk	

Roll out two-thirds of the pastry and use to line a 7-inch (18-cm.) flan case. Dissolve the stock cube in the boiling water and place in a saucepan. Add the milk, butter and flour and whisk over a medium heat until smooth and thick. Stir in the chicken and mushrooms. Cool and pour into the pastry case. Roll out the remaining pastry to form a lid, dampen the edges and seal well together but do not cut a steam vent.

To freeze Place in a polythene bag. Seal and label.

To serve Unwrap and cut a steam vent. Brush with beaten egg and bake in a hot oven (425°F, 220°C, Gas Mark 7) for 30 minutes.

Pineapple castles

4 oz./100 g. butter
4 oz./100 g. sugar
2 eggs
4 tablespoons milk

8 oz./225 g. self-raising
   flour
6 tablespoons chopped
   fresh pineapple

Cream the butter and sugar until fluffy. Beat the eggs into the milk and add to the creamed mixture alternately with the flour, a little at a time. Thickly butter six individual foil moulds and put a spoonful of chopped pineapple in each. Fill with the sponge mixture and bake in a hot oven (425°F, 220°C, Gas Mark 7) for about 20 minutes. Cool.
To freeze Put lids or foil 'hats' on the moulds, seal and label.
To serve Steam from the frozen state for about 45 minutes and serve with cream or pineapple syrup.

Rhubarb and orange cups

1 orange jelly
2 lb./1 kg. rhubarb
2 oranges
6 oz./175 g. sugar

1 pint/6 dl. thick custard
3 egg whites
whipped cream and fresh
   berry fruits to serve

Make up the jelly, according to the directions on the packet and divide between the bases of 12 freezerproof dessert dishes; allow to set. Trim and cut the rhubarb into short lengths. Grate the zest from the oranges and squeeze the juice. Cook the rhubarb in the orange juice with the sugar, until tender. Cool, sieve or liquidise, and stir in the orange zest. Blend the fruit purée with the custard. Beat the egg whites until stiff, fold into the mixture and pour over the jellies. Allow to set.
To freeze Cover or seal, and label.
To serve Remove the cover or seal, defrost and decorate with piped rosettes of whipped cream, and top with fresh berry fruits as available.
Note With a dozen of these you can use them up a few at a time for a party.

Nutty orange bread

2 oz./50 g. walnut
   pieces
2 oz./50 g. candied
   orange peel
12 oz./350 g. self-raising
   flour
½ teaspoon salt

3 oz./75 g. sugar
½ teaspoon grated orange
   zest
2 eggs, beaten
9 tablespoons milk
2 oz./50 g. butter, melted

Finely chop the walnuts and candied peel. Sieve the flour and salt into a mixing bowl, add the walnuts, sugar, peel and grated zest. Mix to a loose doughy consistency with the beaten eggs and milk, beating well. Fold in the melted butter. Pour the mixture into a greased 2-lb. (1-kg.) loaf tin and bake in a moderate oven (350°F, 180°C, Gas Mark 4) for about 1 hour. Turn out and leave to cool on a wire tray.
To freeze Wrap in foil or place in a polythene bag, seal and label.
To serve Defrost at room temperature for about 4 hours and serve sliced and spread with butter.

One-stage Victoria sandwich
(Illustrated)

4 oz./100 g. self-raising
   flour
1 teaspoon baking powder
4 oz./100 g. soft-blend
   margarine

4 oz./100 g. castor sugar
2 eggs, standard

Line the bases of two 7-inch (18-cm.) sandwich tins (or one 8-inch (20-cm.) tin) with a circle of greaseproof paper. Brush the paper and insides of the tins with melted margarine. Sieve the flour and baking powder into a bowl. Add the remaining ingredients and beat the mixture together with a wooden spoon until well mixed and a smooth batter is formed. Place the mixture in the prepared tins and smooth the tops. Bake in a moderate oven (325°F, 160°C, Gas Mark 3) for 25–35 minutes. (Bake one 8-inch (20-cm.) cake for 35–45 minutes.) Turn out and cool on a wire tray.
To freeze Pack in a polythene bag with a foil divider. Seal and label.
To serve Defrost at room temperature for 1 hour. Fill and decorate as liked. Lemon or orange curd (see recipe opposite) makes a good filling.

Cottage cheese, banana and walnut teabread

8-oz./225-g. carton
   cottage cheese, sieved
4 oz./100 g. soft brown
   sugar
3 eggs
2 oz./50 g. walnuts,
   chopped

1 large or 2 small
   bananas, chopped
8 oz./225 g. self-raising
   flour
1 teaspoon baking powder

Cream together the cottage cheese and sugar. Gradually beat in the eggs then stir in the walnuts and banana. Sieve the flour and baking powder together and fold into the mixture. Line a 2-lb. (1-kg.) loaf tin with greaseproof paper and brush with oil. Spoon in the mixture and bake in a moderate oven (350°F, 180°C, Gas Mark 4) for 40–45 minutes, until risen and browned. Leave in the tin for 5 minutes, then turn on to a wire tray and peel off the paper. Cool.
To freeze Wrap in foil or place in a polythene bag. Seal and label.
To serve Allow to defrost completely and serve in slices spread with butter.

Lemon curd
(Illustrated)

2 lemons
8 oz./225 g. castor sugar

3 oz./75 g. butter
3 eggs

Finely grate the zest from the lemons and squeeze the juice. Place the juice, zest and sugar in the top of a double boiler, or basin placed over a pan of hot water, and stir until the sugar has dissolved. Add the butter and allow to melt. Remove from the heat and allow to cool. Beat in the eggs, then return the mixture to the heat and stir constantly, without boiling, until the mixture thickens. Pour into polythene containers; cool, seal, label, and freeze. For immediate use, pour some of the lemon curd into warm jars; cool, seal and cover and store in the refrigerator.

To make *orange curd*, use 2 oranges and the juice of half a lemon.

One-stage Victoria sandwich; lemon curd

Freezing hints

Eggs can be frozen uncooked, but never in the shell as they burst when the water content expands on freezing. Freeze them lightly beaten, breaking each egg into a cup before adding to the bowl to make sure it is fresh. Whisk briefly to blend, without beating in air. Add 1 teaspoon salt or 2 teaspoons sugar to each $\frac{1}{2}$ pint (3 dl.) of egg mixture (about 5 eggs) as a stabiliser. Allow a small headspace and mark the packs for sweet or savoury cooking. Freeze some in ice cube trays to add to sauces, soups, desserts and ice creams. Yolks and whites will freeze separately, yolks as for whole eggs and whites unbeaten and without any additions. Another way of packing eggs for the freezer is to place the beaten yolks in one half of a clean plastic egg box and the beaten whites in the other half. Open freeze until solid, then tape the two halves together.

Egg custards are better frozen before cooking. Open freeze in dishes until solid, tape together in pairs, with a foil divider between the custard surfaces for storage. To serve, separate and cook, from the frozen state, in a bain marie, in a moderately hot oven (400°F, 200°C, Gas Mark 6) for 30–40 minutes, according to size. Cooked savoury custard flans containing bacon, ham, onions, mushrooms, cheese, smoked fish or shellfish can be frozen. Place the cooked savoury ingredients in the base of the flan case, pour seasoned custard over, open freeze, cover with foil and store. Bake from the frozen state in a moderately hot oven (400°F, 200°C, Gas Mark 6) for 20 minutes. Remove the foil and cook for another 10 minutes. Alternatively, bake off and cool. Pack, label and seal. To serve, defrost and reheat in a hot oven (425°F, 220°C, Gas Mark 7) for 20 minutes.

Pancakes are versatility itself. Freeze them in piles, with dividers – stuffed, rolled and packed closely together; or spread with a flavoured butter and folded. Basic pancakes can be layered with savoury or sweet sauces, then cut into wedges; or spread out on baking sheets and reheated in a hot oven, to roll and serve with lemon juice and sugar.

When you are having a baking session it is a great saving of time, energy, effort and fuel to make at least double the quantity and store some in the freezer for use at a future date. For example, the nutty orange bread recipe on page 19 can be doubled and baked in greased foil loaf tins if you don't have sufficient baking tins. Even if you do bake the mixture in foil tins it must still be turned out on to a wire tray to cool, otherwise the mixture will steam.

Interleave small items which stick together when frozen, and chill all cooked food quickly before freezing.

Gardening hints

Sow the following in the open:
Broad beans (Masterpiece, Green Longpod, Meteor)
Cauliflower (Improved Snowball, Kangaroo, Barrier Reef Wombat)

Buys of the month

Fish Mackerel, salmon, whitebait, oysters, scallops
Meat, poultry and game New Zealand lamb, chicken, duckling, turkey, plover, snipe, pigeon
Vegetables Horseradish, parsnips, seakale, broccoli, Brussels sprouts, cauliflower, celery
Fruit Pineapple, rhubarb
Miscellaneous Eggs

APRIL

Spinach soup

1 lb./450 g. fresh
   spinach
1½ oz./40 g. butter
½ oz./15 g. cornflour

1 pint/6 dl. chicken stock
1 teaspoon sugar
salt and pepper
pinch grated nutmeg

Cook the spinach in very little water and drain well. Melt the butter in a saucepan and stir in the cornflour. Cook over a gentle heat but do not allow to colour. Gradually add the stock and bring to the boil, stirring constantly. Add the spinach, lower the heat and simmer for about 5 minutes. Add the sugar, salt, pepper and nutmeg. Cool slightly, then liquidise the soup or put it through a Mouli. Cool.

To freeze Pour into a polythene container, seal and label.

To serve Turn the frozen soup into a saucepan, add 1 pint (6 dl.) of milk and heat gently. Stir well and adjust seasoning if necessary. Just before serving add a swirl of cream, if liked.

Pigeon pâté

3 pigeons
scant ¼ pint/1 dl. vinegar
generous ¼ pint/2 dl. red
   wine
½ teaspoon ground nutmeg
½ teaspoon dried thyme

1 bay leaf
salt and pepper to taste
2 onions, chopped
8 oz./225 g. sausagemeat
1 thick slice brown bread

Cut each pigeon into four joints and place in a shallow dish. To make the marinade, mix together the vinegar, wine, nutmeg, thyme, bay leaf, seasoning and onions. Pour over the pigeons, cover and leave in the refrigerator for 2–3 days. Cut the meat from the bones and chop finely or mince. Mix in the sausagemeat and bread, soaked in the marinade. Blend thoroughly, then press into a greased pâté dish, loaf tin or shaped foil container. Cover with foil and place in a baking tin half filled with water. Cook in a moderate oven (350°F, 180°C, Gas Mark 4) for 1½ hours. Cool.

To freeze Cover the dish with moulded foil and smooth down the edges. Seal and label.

To serve Uncover and defrost at room temperature for 4 hours, or turn out while frozen and defrost on a serving dish. (This recipe will give 8 servings as a starter.)

Note The container may be lined with stretched rashers of streaky bacon, instead of greasing it, before pressing in the mixture.

First blossom chicken

2 tablespoons soy sauce	4 oz./100 g. mushrooms
3 tablespoons oil	2 oz./50 g. fresh
salt and pepper	spinach leaves
1 clove garlic, crushed	¼ pint/1½ dl. chicken
pinch ground ginger	stock
4 chicken breasts	2 teaspoons cornflour

Mix together the soy sauce, 1 tablespoon of the oil, the salt, pepper, garlic and ginger. Brush this all over the chicken breasts and refrigerate them overnight in a closed container. Heat the remaining oil and use to fry the chicken breasts for 5 minutes on each side. Cover the pan and cook over a low heat for a further 15 minutes, adding any remaining marinade for the last 5 minutes of cooking time. Remove the chicken breasts to a shaped foil container. Slice the mushrooms and shred the spinach leaves. Add the stock to the pan juices and bring to the boil. Add the mushrooms and spinach leaves and simmer for 2 minutes. Moisten the cornflour with 2 tablespoons of water, add to the pan and stir over the heat until the sauce thickens and clears. Pour the sauce over the chicken and leave to cool.

To freeze Cover with a lid or foil, seal and label.
To serve Defrost and then reheat in a moderately hot oven (375°F, 190°C, Gas Mark 5) for 25–30 minutes.

Duck with orange and cherry sauce
(Illustrated)

1 5-lb./2¼-kg. fresh duck	few strips orange rind
¼ pint/1½ dl. giblet stock	1 8-oz./225-g. can red
1 tablespoon port	cherries
juice of 1 orange	1 tablespoon cornflour
few drops Tabasco sauce	

Place the prepared duck on a trivet in a roasting pan and cook in a moderately hot oven (400°F,

200°C, Gas Mark 6) for 2 hours, basting the duck occasionally with the pan juices. Remove the duck and carve it into portions; place in foil containers. Remove the fat from the roasting pan and pour the cooking juices into a pan. Add the stock, port, orange juice and Tabasco sauce. Cook for 1 minute. Add the strips of orange rind, drained cherries and cornflour blended with 2 tablespoons of syrup from the can of cherries. Stir over a moderate heat until the sauce is smooth and thickened. Ladle over the duck in the foil containers. Cool.

To freeze Cover with pieces of freezer film to prevent air reaching any exposed parts of the duck portions. Cover with a lid, seal and label.
To serve Defrost and reheat, uncovered, in a hot oven (425°F, 220°C, Gas Mark 7) for 25 minutes.
Note This recipe may also be made using a defrosted, frozen duck in which case the duck will not require basting during roasting.

Lamb kebabs

1 lb./450 g. lean leg of	1 clove garlic, crushed
lamb	1 teaspoon ground
Marinade	coriander
2 tablespoons olive oil	**To serve**
2 tablespoons wine	2 green peppers
vinegar	1 onion, quartered
salt and pepper to taste	16 button mushrooms

Cut the lamb into neat cubes. Mix together the ingredients for the marinade and place in a polythene container. Add the cubes of meat and turn in the marinade.

To freeze Seal and label the container.
To serve Defrost in the refrigerator overnight. Seed and cut the pepper flesh into squares. Thread the meat, pepper, onion and mushrooms on four skewers. Brush with the defrosted marinade and grill for 5–8 minutes, turning the skewers frequently and brushing with the marinade.

Duck with orange and cherry sauce

Marinade 1

(Suitable for red meats)

1 carrot	3 bay leaves
2 shallots	3 parsley stalks
2 cloves garlic	sprigs thyme and
½ pint/3 dl. red wine	rosemary
4 tablespoons wine	1½ teaspoons salt
vinegar	6 peppercorns
1 tablespoon corn oil	

Peel and slice the carrot and shallots and crush the garlic. Place all the ingredients in a saucepan and bring slowly to the boil. Simmer for 10 minutes. Cool, then strain and use as a marinade for red meats.

Marinade 2

(Suitable for chicken, pork and lamb)

2 oz./50 g. onion, chopped	2 tablespoons honey
2 tablespoons corn oil	1 bay leaf
2 tablespoons lemon juice	1 sprig thyme
1 tablespoon cider	pinch ground ginger
vinegar	
1 teaspoon	
Worcestershire sauce	

Beat all the ingredients together and use to marinate meat and poultry, and to baste with during cooking.

To freeze marinades Refrigerate pieces of meat in the marinade overnight. Freeze, with the marinade, in polythene containers. Seal and label. Store for a maximum of 3 months.

Fresh fruit fritters

4 oz./100 g. plain flour	slices of fresh pineapple,
2 tablespoons oil	or apple, or firm
2 eggs, separated	banana slices sprinkled
scant ¼ pint/1 dl. water	with lemon juice
	oil for deep frying

Sieve the flour into a bowl and beat in the oil, egg yolks and sufficient water to make a smooth batter. Beat the egg whites stiffly and fold into the mixture. Dip the fruit slices into the batter, then fry in deep hot oil until the batter is crisp but not coloured. Drain well on absorbent kitchen paper and cool.

To freeze Pack with foil dividers in polythene containers or bags. Seal and label.

To serve Fry the fritters from the frozen state in deep hot oil for about 5 minutes, until light golden brown. Drain well and serve dredged with icing sugar.

Rhubarb raisin crumble

1 lb./450 g. rhubarb	6 oz./175 g. flour
1 orange	4 oz./100 g. sugar
4 tablespoons honey	2 oz./50 g. butter,
3 oz./75 g. raisins or	softened
sultanas	

Chop the rhubarb finely and put into a shaped foil pie dish. Grate the zest from the orange and squeeze the juice. Add these to the rhubarb with the honey and raisins or sultanas. Stir well. To make the crumble topping, mix together the flour, sugar and softened butter. Spread the crumble mixture over the rhubarb and pat it firmly with the back of a wooden spoon.

To freeze Put on a lid or cover with foil, seal and label.

To serve Put the frozen crumble into a hot oven (425°F, 220°C, Gas Mark 7) for 20 minutes, then reduce the heat to moderately hot (375°F, 190°C, Gas Mark 5) for a further 1 hour. Serve with cream, ice cream or custard.

Freezing hints

Allow time for a marinade to tenderise the meat before freezing it in the marinade. Strained marinating liquid can be used to baste small cuts of meat and poultry threaded with other ingredients on skewers for kebabs, or as part of the liquid used in a stew. Cooked marinades develop a rich flavour, and can be based on what you have available – wine, vinegar or lemon juice; olive or corn oil; a selection of fresh and dried herbs, spices and chopped root vegetables. Simmer for 10 minutes, cool and strain over the meat, chill and freeze. Use delicate marinades for chicken and white meats, more strongly flavoured ones for red meat.

Chain cooking is worth a try. A whole carton of chicken portions may get boring by the time you reach the last one. Oven bake double the number required for a meal, without added fat, but sprinkling the skin side liberally with soy sauce and Worcestershire sauce. Next day, dice the leftover cold chicken, fold into mayonnaise tinted pink with paprika. Another time, poach the same quantity in chicken stock, serve one meal of poached chicken in a thick lemon sauce made with stock, lemon juice and parsley, on rice. The next day, simmer diced cucumber, raw sweet pepper and onions Chinese-style in more of the stock, thicken with blended cornflour, and pour over the leftover chicken, thinly sliced (reserve the wing portions for this). Serve on a bed of noodles.

Sliced cooked turkey breast can be frozen between dividers for 4 weeks. Serve it spread with liver pâté and defrosted mandarin segments, set in aspic jelly, for parties.

Other types of poultry freeze well in aspic jelly and when defrosted are clear and bright. Duck which is not perfect in appearance (some tend to look scrawny) or duck portions, can be gently cooked in stock instead of roasted. Add bay leaves, peppercorns, parsley stalks and a stock cube to the water and season to taste. Simmer the duck, just covered with stock, in a pan with a well fitting lid until tender. Remove, cool and bone the duck. Skim off the fat from the stock, strain, and clear by bringing to the boil with the lightly beaten white of an egg and the cracked shell. Strain through a fine sieve and stir in sufficient aspic jelly crystals (plus 1 teaspoon gelatine) to set the measured stock. Pour about 1 inch (2·5 cm.) into a small or large shaped foil container according to quantity. Allow to set, then arrange the duck pieces on top; fill level with cooked peas, then pour on the rest of the aspic. When set, cover and freeze. The mould turns out easily when defrosted, or can be dipped in hot water for 30 seconds to help it turn out. Serve on a bed of salad.

Make sure airtight seals are really airtight, or tape round with freezer tape.

Gardening hints

Sow the following in the open:
Dwarf French beans (The Prince, Sprite, Mont d'Or Golden Butter)
Peas (Show Perfection, Miracle, Chieftan, Little Marvel, Hurst Beagle)
Mange tout (Carouby de Maussane)
Sweetcorn (First of All, North Star, Earliking, Kelvedon Glory, Early Xtra Sweet)

Buys of the month

Fish Mackerel, halibut, whitebait, plaice, trout, salmon, prawns, crab
Meat, poultry and game English lamb and pork, capon, chicken, duck, duckling, guinea fowl, pigeon
Vegetables Broccoli, carrots, parsnips, cauliflower, spinach, aubergines
Fruit Pineapple, rhubarb

MAY

Cream of asparagus soup

1 lb./450 g. thin asparagus or sprue	1 chicken stock cube
1½ oz./40 g. butter	1 egg yolk
1 oz./25 g. flour	4 tablespoons single cream

Clean the asparagus well and cook in plenty of boiling, lightly salted water, until tender. Drain the asparagus (reserve the cooking liquor), trim off the stringy lower part of the stalks, and roughly chop the tips. Melt the butter, stir in the flour and cook gently for 1 minute. Dissolve the stock cube in 1 pint (6 dl.) of the asparagus water and gradually add to the pan, stirring constantly. Bring to the boil, and stir over a low heat until slightly thickened and smooth. Add the chopped asparagus. (If preferred, liquidise or sieve the asparagus tips first.) Lightly beat the egg yolk and cream together. Add a few tablespoons of hot soup to this mixture, stir well and return to the pan. Stir sufficiently to combine, remove from the heat and cool.

To freeze Pour into a polythene container, seal and label.

To serve Turn the frozen soup into a saucepan and reheat gently until hot but not boiling, stirring frequently.

Note In this soup the cream and egg form a liaison, to prevent curdling during storage.

Noisettes of lamb
(Illustrated)

4 frozen noisettes of lamb	4 slices stale white bread
salt and pepper	2 tablespoons corn oil
2 oz./50 g. butter	watercress

Put the defrosted noisettes in the grill pan and season with salt and pepper. Put a small knob of butter on each noisette and grill for 5 minutes on each side, basting with the juices in the pan. Meanwhile, cut 4 croûtes from the bread slices, with a biscuit cutter. Heat the oil and remaining butter together in a pan and use to fry the croûtes until golden brown on both sides. Drain on absorbent paper. Serve the noisettes on the croûtes and garnish with watercress.

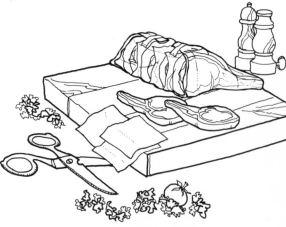

Noisettes of lamb; courgettes dorées (see recipe overleaf)

Smoked haddock in onion milk

½ pint/3 dl. milk
1 onion, chopped
1 large smoked haddock

pepper to taste
1½ oz./40 g. butter
1 teaspoon cornflour

Heat the milk to boiling point, add the onion and leave to stand for 10 minutes. Meanwhile, trim the haddock so it fits a shallow round pan with a lid, put it in, skin side down and cover with water. Bring to the boil, pour off the water and add the strained milk and pepper to taste. Dot with butter, cover the pan and poach over a low heat until just tender. Remove the haddock and divide into portions. Mix the cornflour with 2 table-spoons water in a small pan. Strain in the poaching liquid from the other pan, and stir over a gentle heat until just thickened. Cool.

To freeze Place the haddock portions in individual containers, or freeze all together in a larger, shaped foil container and pour over the sauce. Cover with foil, seal and label.

To serve Uncover, defrost, sprinkle with grated cheese and reheat in a moderate oven (350°F, 180°C, Gas Mark 4) for 20 minutes.

Alternatively, divide the portions between four boiling/freezing bags, and seal. To serve, place the frozen bags in a saucepan of boiling water for 20 minutes. Empty on to hot plates.

Haddock omelettes

1 portion smoked
   haddock in onion milk
   (see previous recipe)
butter

8 eggs
pepper
2 oz./50 g. Gouda
   cheese, grated

Reheat the portion of smoked haddock in onion milk. Discard the skin and flake the fish. Grease the base of an omelette pan with butter. Lightly beat 2 eggs with 1 tablespoon cold water and season with pepper. Make the omelette in the usual way, sprinkle with a little flaked haddock and grated cheese, fold over and turn on to a hot plate. Make three other similar omelettes.

Courgettes dorées

(Illustrated on page 29)

3 lb./1½ kg. courgettes
3 tablespoons corn oil
2 cloves garlic
4 oz./100 g. onion, grated
1 tablespoon soft brown
   sugar

3 tablespoons tomato
   purée
¼ pint/1½ dl. boiling
   water
salt and pepper

Trim both ends of the courgettes. Remove part of the peel in a decorative pattern, and cut the courgettes into 1-inch (2·5-cm.) chunks. Toss in the hot oil for 1 minute; add the crushed garlic, grated onion, sugar, tomato purée blended with the boiling water, and seasoning. Cover and simmer for 10 minutes, stirring occasionally, or until just tender. Cool.

To freeze Freeze in polythene containers or bags. Seal and label. For long term storage omit the garlic and add it at the reheating stage.

To serve Turn, still frozen, into a saucepan and reheat over a gentle heat, stirring from time to time.

Pineapple and mint sorbet

4 thick slices fresh
   pineapple
¼ pint/1½ dl. water
6 oz./175 g. sugar

small bunch mint
1 tablespoon lemon juice
2 egg whites

Remove the peel and core from the pineapple slices and chop the flesh finely. Bring the water and sugar to the boil, slowly, stirring until all the sugar has dissolved. Boil for 3 minutes and cool. Strip the mint leaves from the stalks and wash carefully. Place the mint leaves and pineapple in a blender, pour over the syrup and liquidise until smooth. Add the lemon juice, pour into a shallow container and freeze until mushy. Liquidise again, fold in the stiffly beaten egg whites and freeze until firm in a polythene container. Seal and label.

To serve Serve from the frozen state in individual glass dishes and decorate with fresh mint leaves if available.

Ginger brownies

4 oz./100 g. butter	1 teaspoon ground ginger
8 oz./225 g. soft brown sugar	½ teaspoon baking powder
2 eggs	pinch salt
4 oz./100 g. plain flour	little castor sugar
1½ oz./40 g. cocoa powder	

Cream the butter and sugar together until fluffy then add the eggs, one at a time, beating well. Sieve the flour, cocoa powder, ground ginger, baking powder and salt together and fold into the creamed mixture. Grease a baking tray, about 7 inches (18 cm.) by 11 inches (28 cm.), and spread the mixture in it. Bake in a moderately hot oven (375°F, 190°C, Gas Mark 5) for 30 minutes, until firm to the touch. Sprinkle with castor sugar while still warm and cut into squares. Cool.

To freeze Pack with dividers in polythene containers or bags, seal and label.

To serve Allow to defrost in the pack at room temperature for about 3 hours.

Freezing hints

Freezing small cuts of meat can result in a solid block, unless dividers are used to separate them. A large sheet of freezer film can be folded back and forth, concertina fashion between the cuts, but it is more economical to use up small pieces of foil or freezer film as separate dividers. Make up family-size packs (4 rump steak portions, 8 small chops or whatever suits your family) so you never need to defrost more than one meal. Odd shapes (chump chops, chicken portions) can be moulded in foil or freezer film, then packed in large polythene containers or bags. The secret is to exclude the air around each portion, then enclose again for added protection.

Croûtons add a professional looking garnish to fried dishes, grills, casseroles and soups. Use slightly stale white bread slices and cut them in various shapes and sizes – from ½-inch (1-cm.) cubes to large triangles, or crescent shapes. These are made with a round biscuit cutter, moving it along to produce several new-moon and leaf shapes from each circle. Fry the shapes in a mixture of oil and butter, until an even golden brown. Drain on absorbent paper and cool. Pack in polythene containers. Croûtons do not stick together when frozen. Store for a maximum of 6 weeks.

Chop 2 teacups of mint leaves, mix with 2 tablespoons castor sugar and sufficient vinegar to moisten thoroughly. Pour into ice cube trays and freeze. Turn out and pack in a polythene bag or mould each cube in foil and pack the cubes in a container. To make instant mint sauce, add one or two cubes to a little boiling water and stir well. (If the mint leaves are blanched before freezing they keep a better colour.) Store for a maximum of 9 months.

Use moisture-vapour-proof containers or wrapping material with an airtight seal to protect food against dehydration by the cold, dry air in the freezer cabinet.

Gardening hints

Sow the following in the open:
Courgettes (F1 Hybrid)
Carrots (Early Nantes, Chantenay Red, Cored Supreme, Champion Scarlet Horn)

Buys of the month

Fish Haddock, halibut, plaice, herring, trout, salmon, lobster, prawns, shrimps, crab
Meat, poultry and game English lamb, capon, chicken, duck, duckling, guinea fowl, pigeon
Vegetables Asparagus, broccoli, carrots, cauliflower, new potatoes, green peppers, spinach, courgettes
Fruit Pineapple, rhubarb

JUNE

French apple flan
(Illustrated)

12 oz./350 g. flan pastry	juice of 2 lemons
½ pint/3 dl. apple purée	2 tablespoons apricot jam
3 red-skinned apples	2 tablespoons clear honey

Roll out the pastry and use to line a 9-inch (23-cm.) flan ring. Prick the base and bake blind in a moderately hot oven (375°F, 190°C, Gas Mark 5) for 5 minutes. Cool, then spread the apple purée in the base of the partly-baked flan case. Core and slice the apples, toss the slices in half the lemon juice and arrange them over the apple purée. Return the flan to the oven for a further 20–25 minutes. Allow to cool. Heat the jam, honey and remaining lemon juice until syrupy, but do not allow to boil. Press through a sieve and spoon over the apples to glaze them.
To freeze Open freeze, then wrap in foil. Seal and label.
To serve Unwrap and defrost at room temperature.

Apricot chiffon
(Illustrated)

½ pint/3 dl. apple purée	1 oz./25 g. gelatine
1-lb. 13-oz./825-g. can apricot halves	¼ pint/1½ dl. double cream
2 egg yolks	3 egg whites

Place the apple purée in a bowl. Drain the apricot halves and liquidise or sieve the fruit. Add to the apple purée and beat in the egg yolks. Dissolve the gelatine in a little hot water, cool and stir into the fruit purée. Whip the cream lightly and fold into the mixture together with the stiffly beaten egg whites. Divide the mixture between individual containers, or pour into one large container.
To freeze Cover with foil, seal and label.
To serve Uncover and defrost at room temperature. Decorate with an apricot half and sprinkle with a few toasted, flaked almonds.
Note When stewing summer fruits, store some in heat-sealed bags for future use in purées.

French apple flan; apricot chiffon

Gooseberry party mousse

½ pint/3 dl. sieved gooseberry purée
sugar to taste
few drops green food colouring
½ oz./15 g. gelatine
½ pint/3 dl. double cream
3 egg whites

Sweeten the gooseberry purée to taste and tint it a pale green with a few drops of green food colouring. Dissolve the gelatine in 2 tablespoons water in a small basin over a pan of hot water. Stir into the fruit purée. When mixture begins to thicken, whip the cream and fold it in. Beat the egg whites until stiff and fold in until well blended. Divide the mixture between individual soufflé dishes or containers, or pour into one large dish.
To freeze Cover with foil, seal and label.
To serve Uncover and defrost at room temperature for about 3 hours. Decorate with whipped cream rosettes and pistachio nuts or toasted almonds.

Black cherry pudding

2–3 lb./1–1½ kg. sweet black cherries
granulated sugar to taste
thin slices white bread
butter

Wash and stone cherries and cook over a gentle heat with the sugar. Remove from the heat and allow to cool. Spread the bread slices with butter and remove the crusts. Put a layer of cherries in a round dish or shaped foil container and cover with the buttered bread slices. Repeat in layers, finishing with bread, buttered side up.
To freeze Cover with a lid or foil, seal and label.
To serve Turn out on a serving dish when just defrosted – the pudding will be jellified. Serve with whipped cream.

Crab in cream

1 oz./25 g. butter
1 oz./25 g. flour
½ pint/3 dl. milk
8 oz./225 g. crabmeat, fresh or frozen
1 tablespoon sherry
½ teaspoon Dijon mustard
salt and pepper
juice of ½ lemon
2 tablespoons cream

Melt the butter in a saucepan, stir in the flour and gradually add the milk over a gentle heat. Bring to the boil, stirring constantly, until the sauce is smooth and thickened. Flake the crabmeat and mix into the sauce with the sherry, mustard, salt and pepper, lemon juice and cream. Cool.
To freeze Pack in polythene containers, seal and label; or in scallop shells (see page 39).
To serve Turn the frozen mixture into a saucepan and heat gently. Add more cream if the mixture is too dry. Serve on triangles of buttered toast as a starter or savoury, or as a filling for vol-au-vents.

Beefy pepperpots

½ oz./15 g. butter
8 oz./225 g. minced beef
4 large green peppers
4 oz./100 g. cooked ribbon noodles
2 tablespoons chopped parsley
1 teaspoon dried thyme
1 tablespoon lemon juice
salt and pepper
2 tablespoons olive oil

Melt the butter and use to fry the minced beef until lightly browned. Cut the peppers in half lengthwise and remove the seeds and membrane. Mix the noodles with the meat, parsley, thyme, lemon juice, seasoning and half the oil. Pile this mixture into the pepper halves. Well grease a shaped foil container with the remainder of the oil, place the peppers in the dish and cover with foil. Bake in a moderate oven (325°F, 160°C, Gas Mark 3) for 1 hour. Cool.
To freeze Seal and label.
To serve Uncover, dot with butter and a little grated cheese, re-cover with the foil and place in a moderate oven for about 45 minutes.

Freezing hints

Apples begin appearing with the arrival of Australian Granny Smiths which are good for freezing puréed or sliced. Slices stay white if dropped into salt water until a batch is ready to drain, pack and cover. Or, steam-blanch slices for 1 minute only. Another idea is to dip slices, as prepared, into lemon juice, or pack them covered with a weak ascorbic acid solution. Add a pinch of the crystals to each $\frac{1}{4}$ pint ($1\frac{1}{2}$ dl.) water, enough for a 16-oz. (450-g.) container. Later on, when Bramleys and other home-grown apples come in, use up windfalls first in the form of purée, cutting out all the damaged parts.

The same treatment applies to other fruit which discolour, such as peaches, apricots, and later greengages and plums. But do not blanch these; they are better stoned (as the stones give a bitter flavour during storage) and packed in a medium strength sugar syrup. 11 oz. (300 g.) sugar dissolved in 1 pint (6 dl.) water gives a 40% syrup. Use chilled and leave at least a $\frac{1}{2}$-inch (1-cm.) headspace in the container and place a crumpled piece of foil in this headspace to keep the fruit under the surface of the syrup. This prevents the fruit rising as it freezes and parts exposed to the air inside the pack turning brown.

Herbs, if well washed and free from grit, can be frozen unblanched. Pack in small quantities, in flat foil packs well crimped together, or polythene containers (2-oz. (50-g.) Tupperware tumblers are ideal). If possible, freeze parsley leaves and stalks in separate packs, as leaves can be crumbled while still frozen inside the pack, and stalks are useful to flavour marinades or stews. Other fresh herbs can be treated like mint and frozen in cubes, but not those with woody stems like rosemary, which is better dried.

Use all last year's fruit and vegetables before freezing down this year's crop.

Gardening hints

Sow the following in the open:
Runner beans (Achievement, Enorma, Prizewinner, Kelvedon Marvel)

Buys of the month

Fish Haddock, plaice, whitebait, trout, salmon, salmon trout, lobster, prawns, shrimps, crab, crayfish
Meat, poultry and game English lamb, capon, chicken, duck, duckling, guinea fowl, pigeon
Vegetables Asparagus, broccoli, carrots, cauliflower, courgettes, peas, new potatoes, peppers, spinach
Fruit Apples (imported), apricots, cherries, peaches, pineapple, gooseberries, raspberries, strawberries

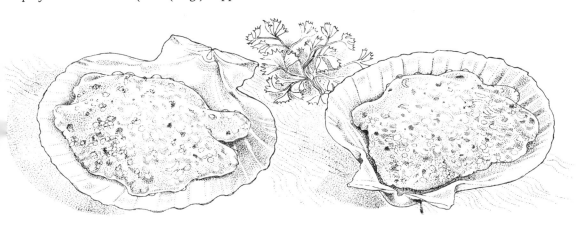

JULY

Green pea soup

1 onion	3 pints/1½ litres chicken
1 small lettuce	stock
2 sprigs mint	2 teaspoons sugar
1 oz./25 g. butter	salt and pepper
2 lb./1 kg. peas	

Grate the onion, finely shred the lettuce and chop the mint. Melt the butter over gentle heat, add the peas, onion, lettuce and mint. Cover the pan and cook gently together for 10 minutes. Add the stock, sugar and seasoning and simmer for about 1½ hours. Cool slightly, then liquidise or sieve. Cool.

To freeze Pour into polythene containers, seal and label.

To serve Turn the frozen soup into a saucepan and reheat gently, stirring frequently. Adjust the seasoning and add a swirl of cream to each portion just before serving.

Note Field peas, or elderly garden peas, which would be too tough if served as a vegetable, are ideal for this recipe.

Fresh berry jam
(Illustrated)

2 lb./1 kg. berry fruit*	1 8-oz./225-g. bottle
3½ lb./1¾ kg. castor sugar	commercial pectin
4 tablespoons lemon juice	

Suitable for blackberries, blackcurrants, loganberries, raspberries, redcurrants or strawberries.

Place the prepared fruit, sugar and lemon juice in a bowl. Stir well and allow to stand in a warm place until the sugar has completely dissolved. Stir in the commercial pectin and when the jam begins to set, ladle it into small polythene tumblers or glass jars. Seal and leave in a warm place overnight.

To freeze Label and store in the freezer for a maximum of 6–8 months.

To serve Allow to defrost for 30–45 minutes at room temperature.

Fresh berry jam

Breton shells

8 oz./225 g. white fish
    fillets
salt and pepper
1 bay leaf
$\frac{1}{4}$ pint/1$\frac{1}{2}$ dl. dry cider
2 oz./50 g. butter
2 oz./50 g. onion,
    chopped

4 oz./100 g. mushrooms,
    chopped
2 tablespoons tomato
    purée
4 tablespoons fresh white
    breadcrumbs
4 oz./100 g. prawns or
    shrimps

Lay the fish fillets in a shallow pan, season and add the bay leaf. Pour over the cider, cover and poach gently for 5 minutes. Cool, remove the fish, skin and flake. Reduce the stock by rapid boiling to about half. Melt the butter and use to sauté the onion and mushrooms for 3 minutes. Stir in the tomato purée, breadcrumbs, flaked fish and prawns or shrimps. Strain over the reduced stock and stir well. Divide the mixture between four well buttered, deep scallop shells and place on a baking sheet in a moderately hot oven (375°F, 190°C, Gas Mark 5) for 20 minutes. Cool.

To freeze Cover the exposed surfaces with foil crimped under the shell edges. Open freeze, then pack together in a polythene container. Seal and label.

To serve Remove the foil, sprinkle the surface with breadcrumbs and dot with butter. Place in a hot oven (425°F, 220°C, Gas Mark 7) to defrost and cook for 25 minutes. Store for a maximum of 3 months.

Lamb chop casserole

1 oz./25 g. butter
2 teaspoons oil
4 oz./100 g. button
    onions
4 large lamb chops
3 sticks celery
4 oz./100 g. button
    mushrooms

2 dessert apples
1 oz./25 g. flour
$\frac{3}{4}$ pint/4 dl. chicken
    stock
$\frac{1}{4}$ pint/1$\frac{1}{2}$ dl. cider
salt and pepper

Melt the butter and oil in a flameproof casserole and use to sauté the onions gently for about 3 minutes. Add the chops and sauté until golden brown. Chop the celery, wipe the mushrooms and peel, core and slice the apples. Add these to the pan and cook for about 5 minutes. Stir in the flour until well blended, then gradually add the stock, cider and seasoning, stirring constantly. Cover and cook in a moderately hot oven (375°F, 190°C, Gas Mark 5) for about 45 minutes. Cool.

To freeze Transfer to a shaped foil container, put on a lid or cover with foil, seal and label.

To serve Defrost and then reheat in a moderately hot oven (375°F, 190°C, Gas Mark 5) for 30 minutes, stirring occasionally.

Country currant pies

1 lb./450 g. shortcrust
    pastry
4 oz./100 g. castor sugar

1 lb./450 g. red and
    blackcurrants, mixed

Grease six individual shaped foil containers. Roll out the pastry thinly and cut out 12 circles, each the size of a saucer. Put one circle in each container. Mix together the sugar and fruit and divide between the pastry cases. Dampen the edges of the pastry, put a pastry 'hat' on each pie and seal the edges together well. Decorate with leaves made from pastry trimmings, and brush with a little milk. Bake in a moderately hot oven (375°F, 190°C, Gas Mark 5) for about 30 minutes. Cool.

To freeze Cover each pie with foil, or pack with dividers in a polythene container. Seal and label.

To serve Reheat from the frozen state in a hot oven (450°F, 230°C, Gas Mark 8) for about 20 minutes. Sprinkle with brown sugar before serving with cream or custard.

Wholewheat picnic scones

4 oz./125 g. plain flour
2 teaspoons baking
    powder
4 oz./100 g. wholewheat
    flour

$\frac{1}{4}$ teaspoon salt
2$\frac{1}{2}$ oz./65 g. butter
2 oz./50 g. cheese, grated
$\frac{1}{4}$ pint/1$\frac{1}{2}$ dl. milk

Sieve the plain flour, baking powder and salt together into a bowl. Mix in the wholewheat flour and rub in the butter thoroughly, together with the grated cheese. Mix to a soft dough with the milk and knead lightly. Roll out on a floured board and cut into rounds $\frac{1}{2}$ inch (1 cm.) thick with a pastry cutter. Place on a well greased baking sheet and bake in a hot oven (425°F, 220°C, Gas Mark 7) for about 10 minutes. Cool.

To freeze Pack in a polythene bag or container, seal and label.

To serve Place the frozen scones on a baking sheet, sprinkle with a little grated cheese if liked, and reheat in a hot oven (425°F, 220°C, Gas Mark 7) for 10 minutes. Serve as a picnic accompaniment to a salad.

Freezing hints

The queen of summer fruits, the strawberry, is probably the most difficult fruit to freeze successfully. For the best results, fast-freeze them spread on clean baking sheets or large Tupperware seals. If you feel it necessary to wash strawberries, hull them after they have been open frozen to prevent water filling the stalk space. Each individual fruit should feel firm and solid after 2 hours' open freezing; do not wait for a 'bloom' to appear, as this means the fruit has been too long in the freezer. Pack quickly into rigid-based containers, with foil dividers halfway up. This helps to distribute the weight of the fruit during defrosting when the top layer would press down and squash the softened berries beneath. Serve chilled. Sugar, if added to packs, tends to draw out the juices forming a syrup when defrosted, and detracts from the natural crisp texture. If you use gussetted bags, press a square of clean foil, folded several times, into the base to make the bags firm, square shapes.

Fresh peaches tend to discolour however carefully they are packed for freezing. When peaches are plentiful, cut large ones in half, take out the stones and a little of the pulp. Crush sufficient macaroons to provide a heaped tablespoon per peach. Stir in the scooped-out pulp, sugar to taste and allow a teaspoon of egg yolk and a small nut of butter per peach. Mix all the stuffing ingredients together. Stuff the peach halves with this mixture. Arrange the peaches cut side down in a buttered, shallow, shaped foil container. Pour over a little melted seedless raspberry jam or fresh raspberry syrup and bake in a moderate oven (350°F, 180°C, Gas Mark 4) for 15 minutes. Cool, cover and freeze. When required, defrost, uncover and reheat in a moderate oven for 20 minutes.

Cooked fish dishes look attractive in scallop shells, which fishmongers can supply, and they give adequate freezer protection. Try a simple mixture of flaked white fish folded into a creamy white sauce, flavoured with lemon, mushrooms, or cheese and leave to cool. Spoon the mixture into buttered shells, press a foil cap firmly over the filling, and freeze. To serve, remove the foil, add a quick topping made with instant mashed potato, and bake in a hot oven (425°F, 220°C, Gas Mark 7) for 25 minutes.

Gardening hints

Sow the following in the open:
Beetroot (Suttons Globe, Golden Beet, Detroit-Little Ball)

Buys of the month

Fish Sole, haddock, plaice, trout, salmon trout, eel, lobster, prawns, shrimps, crab, crayfish
Meat, poultry and game English lamb, duck, duckling, guinea fowl
Vegetables French and broad beans, beetroot, broccoli, cauliflower, corn, carrots, courgettes, peas, peppers
Fruit Cherries, figs, gooseberries, seedless grapes, loganberries, peaches, nectarines, raspberries, currants, melons

AUGUST

Shrimp bisque

3 sticks celery

4 oz./100 g. button
  mushrooms

1 small onion

1 carrot

2 oz./50 g. butter

2 pints/generous litre
  chicken stock

salt and pepper

1 teaspoon anchovy paste

2 teaspoons lemon juice

8 oz./225 g. cooked white
  fish

2 tablespoons white wine

8 oz./225 g. shrimps

Finely chop the celery, mushrooms, onions and
carrot. Melt the butter and use to cook the chopped
vegetables gently for about 10 minutes. Add the
stock, seasoning, anchovy paste and lemon juice
and simmer for about 20 minutes. Flake the white
fish and add to the pan. Cool slightly, then
liquidise or sieve the mixture and return to the
pan with the wine and shrimps. Cover and simmer
for 5 minutes. Cool.

To freeze Pack in polythene containers, seal and
label.

To serve Reheat gently over boiling water in a
double boiler, stirring occasionally (or put in a
basin over a pan of hot water). When hot, stir in ½
pint (3 dl.) cream, and continue to heat, but do not
allow to boil.

Note As an alternative other shellfish, such as
flaked crab or lobster meat or coarsely chopped
prawns, may be used.

Dressed bean salad
(Illustrated)

1 clove garlic

½ teaspoon mild
  continental mustard

½ teaspoon salt

½ teaspoon sugar

¼ teaspoon pepper

3 tablespoons wine
  vinegar

6 tablespoons oil

1 lb./½ kg. frozen French
  beans

4 spring onions

Crush the garlic and place in a wide-necked jar
with a lid. Add the seasonings and vinegar and
shake the ingredients together. Add the oil and
shake again. Leave to stand for several hours, or
overnight, to allow the flavours to blend.

Top and tail the beans and string if necessary.
Cook in boiling, salted water until just tender.
Drain and allow to cool. Trim and chop the onions
finely.

To serve Arrange the beans in a serving dish and
sprinkle over the chopped onions. Serve slightly
chilled and sprinkled with the dressing.

Dressed bean salad

Pâté in aspic

2 oz./50 g. butter
4 oz./100 g. fat bacon
2 oz./50 g. onion,
  chopped
1½ lb./¾ kg. chicken livers
½ teaspoon grated nutmeg

¾ teaspoon ground cloves
salt and pepper
2 eggs
fresh tarragon leaves
1 packet aspic jelly
  crystals

Melt the butter in a frying pan and use to cook the diced bacon and chopped onion gently for 5 minutes. Add the livers and cook for a further 10 minutes. Cool slightly, then liquidise, or press the mixture through a sieve. Beat in the seasonings and lightly beaten eggs. Divide the mixture between small foil containers or ramekin dishes. Place the containers in a roasting pan half filled with water and cook in a moderate oven (350°F, 180°C, Gas Mark 4) for 45 minutes. Allow to cool. Place 2 fresh tarragon leaves on the top of each dish. Make up the aspic liquid double strength and pour a ¼-inch (½-cm.) layer over the top of the pâté. Allow to set.

To freeze Cover with foil and smooth down the edges. Seal and label.

To serve Allow to defrost at room temperature for 1 hour. Serve with slices of toast. Store for a maximum of 3 months.

Marrow and tomato scramble

1 medium marrow
2 oz./50 g. butter
1 tablespoon oil
2 large or 3 small onions,
  sliced

1 clove garlic, crushed
1 green pepper
8 large tomatoes
salt and pepper

Peel the marrow, remove the seeds and cut the flesh into small cubes. Melt the butter and oil in a large pan and use to cook the sliced onions and the garlic gently. Seed and slice the pepper finely, add to the onions and cook for a further 5 minutes. Skin and slice the tomatoes and add these to the pan with the marrow. Cook all together gently for about 20 minutes, stirring from time to time. Season well and cool.

To freeze Pack in a polythene container, seal and label.

To serve Turn, still frozen, into a saucepan and heat gently, stirring frequently, until thoroughly warmed through. Beat 4 eggs lightly and stir into the warmed vegetables and cook, stirring constantly, until the eggs are just beginning to set. Pile on buttered toast and serve at once.

Eve's plum pudding

2–3 lb./1–1½ kg. plums
2 tablespoons brown
  sugar
2 tablespoons water
2 oz./50 g. butter

2 oz./50 g. sugar
1 egg
2 tablespoons milk
4 oz./100 g. self-raising
  flour

Halve and stone the plums and put in a saucepan with the brown sugar and water. Stew gently for about 10 minutes, then place in a shaped foil pie dish and set aside. In a warm basin, cream together the butter and sugar. Beat the egg into the milk and add to the creamed mixture, alternately, with the flour, a little at a time. Mix thoroughly, then spread over the plums in the pie dish. Bake in a moderate oven (325–350°F, 160–180°C, Gas Mark 3–4) for about 40 minutes. Cool.

To freeze Cover with foil, seal and label.

To serve Sprinkle the frozen surface with brown sugar and dot with butter before reheating in a hot oven (425°F, 220°C, Gas Mark 7) for about 30 minutes. Serve with cream or custard.

Viennese hazelnut cake

4 oz./100 g. butter
4 oz./100 g. castor sugar
1 tablespoon flour
4 standard eggs,
  separated
4 oz./100 g. hazelnuts,
  ground

4 oz./100 g. plain
  chocolate
2 tablespoons strong
  black coffee

Cream the butter and sugar until fluffy. Add the sieved flour a little at a time, alternately with the egg yolks. Stir in the ground hazelnuts. Melt the chocolate in the coffee in a basin over hot water and beat into the mixture. Beat the egg whites stiffly and fold in. Pour the mixture into a greased 8-inch (20-cm.) cake tin and bake in a cool oven (275°F, 140°C, Gas Mark 1) for about 1½ hours, or until the cake feels resilient when tested with a fingertip. Cool.

To freeze Pack in a polythene bag, seal and label.
To serve Defrost at room temperature for 3 hours and serve with whipped cream.
Note Use hazelnuts with their skins on for this recipe.

Freezing hints

Blanching is a tiresome preliminary to the freezing of vegetables, but it does mean the messy preparation and most of the cooking is already done when it comes to serving them. Blanching also makes vegetables go limp, therefore easier to pack down closely. It also intensifies their bright, fresh colour. Accuracy in timing is essential, since underblanching may fail to halt the enzyme action which causes them to deteriorate while frozen, and overblanching makes the defrosted vegetables flabby. Follow the chart on page 6. As a guide peas take the least time of all – 1–1½ minutes; whole French beans, diced carrots and cauliflower florets 3 minutes; large Brussels sprouts 4 minutes. Blanch 1 lb. (½ kg.) vegetables at a time, in at least 8 pints (4½ litres) fast boiling water. Time the blanching from the moment the water returns to the boil. A light collapsible blancher (shown in the picture on page 41) shortens this wait and makes the whole operation quicker. Replace the blanching water frequently. Exceptions to the rule are as follows: mushrooms need only be wiped clean and dried, although packing them raw does leave awkward airspaces around the mushrooms for them to dehydrate into; sweet red and green peppers can be frozen whole or sliced, with stalk and seeds and white pith removed. Although not exceptions, root vegetables for stews (onion, carrot, swede, parsnip, turnip) can be frozen separately or in mixed packs, without blanching. However, they need to be used within 3 months.

Gardening hints

Sow the following in the open:
Winter spinach (Suttons Greenmarket, Sigmaleaf, Virkade)

Buys of the month

Fish Plaice, sole, turbot, eel, trout, salmon, prawns, shrimps, crab, crayfish
Meat and game Scottish and Welsh lamb, grouse, venison, hare, wild duck
Vegetables French and runner beans, beetroot, horseradish, marrow, peppers, corn, spinach, tomatoes, cauliflower
Fruit Apples, garden blackberries, blackcurrants, seedless grapes, plums, greengages, loganberries, peaches, pears, melons, coconuts

SEPTEMBER

Steak and pigeon casserole

2 pigeons
8 oz./225 g. stewing
  steak
4 oz./100 g. bacon
½ oz./15 g. butter
½ pint/3 dl. stock
4 oz./100 g. mushrooms,
  sliced

salt and pepper
1 tablespoon redcurrant
  jelly
2 tablespoons sherry
1 tablespoon lemon juice
1 tablespoon cornflour

Cut the pigeons in half, cut the stewing steak into small pieces and dice the bacon. Melt the butter in a large frying pan and use to cook the pigeons, steak and bacon until coloured. Turn all into an ovenproof casserole and add the stock, mushrooms and seasoning. Cook in a moderate oven (325°F, 160°C, Gas Mark 3) for about 1 hour. Mix together the redcurrant jelly, sherry, lemon juice and cornflour until well blended. Add to the casserole and stir well. Continue to cook for a further 30 minutes. Cool.

To freeze Pack in a polythene container, seal and label.

To serve Defrost and then reheat in a saucepan over a gentle heat, stirring occasionally. Serve sprinkled with chopped parsley.

Rich tomato sauce
(Illustrated)

2 lb./1 kg. ripe tomatoes
8 oz./225 g. onion,
  chopped
2 teaspoons dried thyme
1 bay leaf
¼ pint/1½ dl. water

2 oz./50 g. butter
1 oz./25 g. cornflour
2 tablespoons finely
  chopped gherkin
salt and pepper

Roughly chop the tomatoes and place in a large saucepan with the onion, thyme, bay leaf and water. Cover and simmer gently until the tomatoes are very soft. Cool slightly, then liquidise or press through a sieve. Melt the butter in a pan, stir in the cornflour and cook for 1 minute without browning. Gradually stir in the tomato purée and gherkin. Bring to the boil, stirring constantly, and simmer for 2 minutes. Adjust the seasoning and leave to cool.

To freeze Place in polythene containers, seal and label.

To serve Turn, still frozen, into a saucepan and reheat gently, stirring to prevent sticking.

Rich tomato sauce

My beef stew

4 lb./1¾ kg. stewing
  steak
2 large green peppers
4 oz./100 g. dripping
2 lb./1 kg. onions, sliced
1 lb./450 g. carrots, sliced
8 oz./225 g. tender prunes
1 teaspoon dried mixed
  herbs

4 oz./100 g. flour
2 beef stock cubes
2 tablespoons tomato
  purée
1 lb./450 g. small
  mushrooms
salt and pepper

Cut the meat into 1-inch (2·5-cm.) cubes and seed and chop the peppers. Melt the dripping in a large frying pan and use to fry the onions, carrots and peppers gently until softened. Add the meat and stir over a high heat to seal. Drain, remove to a casserole, add the prunes and sprinkle over the herbs. Stir the flour into the fat remaining in the pan and cook, stirring constantly, until slightly browned. Gradually add the stock cubes made up to 2 pints (generous litre) with boiling water, and the tomato purée. Bring to the boil, stirring all the time, and cook for 2 minutes. Pour into the casserole. Cover and cook in a moderate oven (325°F, 160°C, Gas Mark 3) for 2½ hours. Add the mushrooms, stir and return to the oven for a further 15 minutes. Adjust the seasoning. Cool.

To freeze Divide the stew between three polythene containers. Seal and label.

To serve Turn the contents into a saucepan, add a little water or stock and reheat gently, stirring occasionally. Store for a maximum of 4 months. Gives 3 servings for 4 people.

Note This stew is much improved by replacing ½ pint (3 dl.) of the stock with red wine.

Cucumber and herb flan

Pastry
6 oz./175 g. plain flour
½ teaspoon baking powder
pinch salt
4 oz./100 g. white
  vegetable fat
2 tablespoons very cold
  water
½ teaspoon vinegar

Filling
4 oz./100 g. cucumber
2 eggs
salt and pepper
2 tablespoons cottage
  cheese
1 tablespoon corn oil
3 oz./75 g. Cheddar
  cheese, grated
pinch dried mixed herbs
little grated cheese to
  sprinkle

Knead together the pastry ingredients to make a ball. Dust with flour and leave overnight in the refrigerator, or wrap and freeze until required. Roll out and use to line a greased 8-inch (20-cm.) pie plate. Peel and dice the cucumber. Lightly beat the eggs with salt and pepper to taste. Mix in the cottage cheese, oil, grated cheese and herbs and blend well. Arrange the cucumber on the pastry-lined plate and pour over the cheese mixture. Sprinkle with a little more cheese and cook in a moderate oven (350°F, 180°C, Gas Mark 4) for 45 minutes. Cool.

To freeze Wrap in foil or a polythene bag, seal and label.

To serve Defrost and serve cold, or reheat in a moderately hot oven (375°F, 190°C, Gas Mark 5) for 20–25 minutes. Serve hot as a main dish with salads, or as a supper dish.

Blackberry crumble cake

1½ lb./¾ kg. blackberries
8 oz./225 g. brown sugar
3 oz./75 g. butter
6 oz./175 g. self-raising
  flour

2 oz./50 g. granulated
  sugar
1 egg, beaten
a little milk

Put the blackberries, layered with the brown sugar, in a shaped foil dish, or pie plate. Rub the butter into the flour and add the granulated sugar,

beaten egg and just sufficient milk to give a fairly stiff cake mixture. Spread this over the black-berries and bake in a moderate oven (350°F, 180°C, Gas Mark 4) for about 40 minutes. Cool.

To freeze Cover with foil, seal and label.

To serve Defrost at room temperature for about 2 hours, then reheat in a moderate oven (350°F, 180°C, Gas Mark 4) for about 35 minutes. Serve with thick cream.

Pear dumplings

4 medium pears	1 egg
2 oz./50 g. brown sugar	1 tablespoon water
few sultanas	
1 lb./450 g. shortcrust pastry	

Choose ripe, but firm, pears. Peel and core them; stuff the centres with brown sugar and a few sultanas. Divide the pastry into four equal pieces, and roll out into circles, each one large enough to enclose a pear. Put each pear on a pastry circle, dampen the pastry edges and fold up round the pear, sealing well. Beat the egg into the water and use to brush the pear parcels completely. Place on a greased baking sheet and bake in a moderate oven (350°F, 180°C, Gas Mark 4) for about 40 minutes. Cool.

To freeze Wrap each dumpling completely in foil, then place together in a polythene bag or container. Seal and label.

To serve Reheat in the foil packs in a hot oven (450°F, 230°C, Gas Mark 8) for 30 minutes. Stick an angelica 'stalk' in the top of each one and serve with cream or custard.

Freezing hints

A big stew is the best illustration of the king-size approach to cooking for the freezer. Multiply the amount for an average meal by three and you have one stew to serve the same day and two to freeze down for a future date. If you cook a similar quantity of another main dish at the same session, you can put a meal for the following day in the refrigerator, and solve your menu problems for two days running – with the bonus of four meals to come out of your freezer later.

Tomatoes are in season now, so make the second choice in your cook-up a goulash, rich with tomatoes, onions and paprika. Use large cubes of stewing beef or pork, or a mixture of both.

American housewives find it easier to prepare a big stew fully, but stop short of cooking and freeze at that point. The stew is defrosted and cooked in the oven, which takes about 3 hours. The oven is only in use once which is definitely an advantage. Try cooking diced shoulder of lamb, onion, carrot, parsnip, sweet pepper, caraway seeds, seasoning and a dash of Tabasco sauce together with stock, and freeze.

Make a fruit salad for the freezer now. Peeled grapes, sliced fresh peaches, apples and pears and melon balls all blend well into a syrup provided by a small can apricots, sliced. Add bananas, sliced, when the fruit salad is defrosting.

Instead of freezing damaged or over-ripe fruit whole, remove the damaged parts then cook the fruit and freeze in containers as a purée.

Buys of the month

Fish 2nd-season mackerel, halibut, haddock, turbot, sole, plaice, trout, lobster, prawns, shrimps, crab, oysters

Meat, poultry and game Beef, chicken, duck, goose, turkey, grouse, pheasant, hare, venison, guinea fowl, pigeon, wild duck

Vegetables Aubergines, runner beans, beetroot, broccoli, courgettes, leeks, marrow, onion, peppers, spinach, swedes, parsnips, tomatoes

Fruit Apples, bilberries, wild blackberries, damsons, greengages, plums, pears, grapes

OCTOBER

Salmon mousse

(Illustrated)

8 oz./225 g. fresh salmon
½ cucumber
4 fl. oz./1 dl. evaporated
  milk
¾ oz./20 g. flour
¾ oz./20 g. butter

salt and pepper
2 teaspoons gelatine
¼ pint/1½ dl. mayonnaise
few drops Tabasco sauce
1 egg white

Poach the salmon, drain and flake. Peel, and halve the cucumber, lengthways, and scoop out the seeds. Dice the flesh and cook for 5 minutes in salted water. Drain well (reserve the liquid) and liquidise, or press through a sieve. Make the evaporated milk up to ½ pint (3 dl.) with water. Place in a saucepan and whisk in the flour. Add the butter and stir constantly over a gentle heat until the mixture has thickened. Cook for 2 minutes, stirring. Season to taste and leave aside to cool.

Dissolve the gelatine in a little hot liquor used for cooking the cucumber, add to the sauce and beat well. Add the flaked salmon, mayonnaise and Tabasco sauce and mix thoroughly. Beat the egg white until stiff and fold into the fish mixture. Turn into a lightly oiled 1½-pint (1-litre) mould and leave to set in a cool place.

To freeze Cover the mould with foil, smoothing down the edges. Seal and label.

To serve Defrost in the refrigerator. Run a table knife or small palette knife around the edge, dip the mould quickly in hot water and turn on to a serving dish. Garnish with chopped set aspic jelly, cold cooked peas, pieces of pimiento and slices of cucumber.

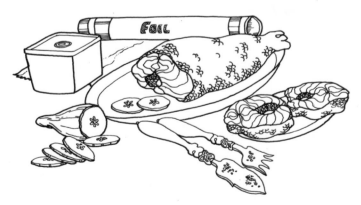

Salmon mousse

Soupe au pistou

2 oz./50 g. haricot beans	4 tablespoons olive oil
4 tomatoes	4 oz./100 g. onion,
8 oz./225 g. French beans	chopped
2 courgettes	salt and pepper
2 small potatoes	

Soak and parboil the haricot beans. Skin and chop the tomatoes. Top, tail and chop the French beans and courgettes. Peel and dice the potatoes. Heat the oil and use to cook the onion gently until transparent. Add the other fresh vegetables, haricot beans and $1\frac{1}{2}$ pints (scant litre) water. Season to taste, bring to the boil, cover and simmer until tender. Cool.

To freeze Ladle into polythene containers, seal and label.

To serve Turn into a pan, defrost over a low heat and add 2 oz. (50 g.) small pasta shapes and simmer for 8 minutes. Meanwhile, crush 2 cloves garlic and pound with 2 tablespoons chopped fresh basil or 1 tablespoon dried. Gradually beat in 3 tablespoons olive oil, drop by drop, until the pistou is a thick consistency like mayonnaise. Stir into the soup just before serving.

Spicy stuffed aubergines

4 large aubergines	$\frac{1}{4}$ teaspoon ground ginger
salt	seasoning
4 tablespoons oil	1 tablespoon tomato
2 large onions	purée
8 oz./225 g. mushrooms	$\frac{1}{2}$ teaspoon sugar
1 clove garlic	
$\frac{1}{4}$ teaspoon ground	
coriander	

Slice the aubergines in half lengthwise. Slash the cut surfaces diagonally about $\frac{1}{2}$ inch (1 cm.) deep, sprinkle with salt and leave to stand for 30 minutes. Rinse off and pat dry with absorbent paper. Heat the oil and use to fry the aubergines very gently, cut side down, for 10–12 minutes. Remove the aubergines from the pan and scoop out as much flesh as possible from the centres. Chop the onions, peel and chop the mushrooms and crush the garlic. Add these to the pan in which the aubergines were cooked and sauté gently until the onion is soft. Stir in the spices and seasoning, tomato purée and sugar and continue cooking over a low heat for a further 2 minutes. Roughly dice the cooked flesh from the aubergines, stir into the pan and pile back into the aubergine shells. Cool.

To freeze Wrap each stuffed aubergine half in foil, seal and label.

To serve Place the foil parcels on a baking sheet and reheat in a moderately hot oven (375°F, 190°C, Gas Mark 5) for 45 minutes.

Tipsy rabbit pudding

8 oz./225 g. lean bacon
    pieces
2 large onions
2 large cooking apples
1 lb./450 g. boneless
    rabbit pieces

8 oz./225 g. suet crust
    pastry
salt and pepper
about ¾ pint/4 dl.
    cider

Cube the bacon, chop the onions and peel, core and chop the apples. Wash the rabbit and put into a large pan of cold water. Bring to the boil and drain. Roll out two-thirds of the pastry and use to line a large, greased shaped foil pudding basin. Fill the pastry case with layers of rabbit, bacon, onion and apple, seasoning each layer well. Add cider barely to cover the filling. Roll out the remaining pastry to form a lid. Dampen the edges and press on lid neatly, sealing well. Make a second loose-fitting 'hat' of double foil and tie this securely over the pudding. Steam for about 4 hours. Cool.

To freeze Pack in a polythene bag, seal and label.

To serve Make a fresh foil cap to cover the frozen pudding and steam for about 1½ hours to reheat.

Spiced gingerbread

12 oz./350 g. plain flour
pinch salt
1½ teaspoons mixed spice
4 teaspoons ground ginger
1 teaspoon grated lemon
    zest
3 oz./75 g. demerara
    sugar
3 oz./75 g. sultanas

6 oz./175 g. butter
3 tablespoons golden
    syrup
3 tablespoons black
    treacle
7 fl. oz./2¼ dl. milk
1½ teaspoons bicarbonate
    of soda
1 egg, beaten

Sieve the flour, salt and spices into a bowl and add the lemon zest. Stir in the demerara sugar and the sultanas. Melt the butter, golden syrup, and black treacle together in a small saucepan over a gentle heat, stirring. Add this to the dry ingredients and beat thoroughly. Slightly warm the milk and in it dissolve the bicarbonate of soda.

Add the egg and pour this into the mixture, beating well. Line a 7-inch (18-cm.) square cake tin with a double layer of foil and butter it well. Pour the mixture into the prepared tin and bake in a moderate oven (350°F, 180°C, Gas Mark 4) for about 45 minutes, until well risen. Cool slightly before removing the gingerbread from the tin, still in the foil. Cool.

To freeze Wrap in foil and a polythene bag, seal and label.

To serve Unwrap and allow to defrost at room temperature for about 4 hours.

Mocha walnut fudge

1½ lb./¾ kg. castor sugar
8 fl. oz./2½ dl.
    evaporated milk
8 fl. oz./2½ dl. cold water
4 oz./100 g. unsalted
    butter

1 tablespoon instant
    coffee powder
1½ teaspoons drinking
    chocolate powder
1 tablespoon water
2 oz./50 g. walnuts

Put the sugar, evaporated milk, water and butter in a large, heavy-based saucepan. Blend the coffee powder and drinking chocolate powder with the water and add to the pan. Heat gently, stirring constantly, until the sugar has dissolved, then bring to the boil, still stirring. Put a sugar thermometer in the pan and continue to boil the mixture gently until the temperature reaches 240°F (116°C). This will take approximately 1–1¼ hours. Stir only occasionally. Remove the pan from the heat when the required temperature is reached and stand it in a container of cold water to hasten cooling. Chop the walnuts and beat them into the mixture with a wooden spoon. Continue beating until the mixture is thick and creamy and just beginning to set. Butter a foil tray about 8 inches (20 cm.) square by 1 inch (2·5 cm.) deep and pour the mixture in. Mark into squares when cool, but do not cut right through.

To freeze Cover the tray with foil, seal and label.

To serve Unwrap and defrost at room temperature for about 1½ hours, then cut through the marked squares.

Freezing hints

Parcel cooking preserves the delicate flavour and juices of fish, and has the added advantage that you freeze and cook the food in the same foil parcel. Enclose the fish steak in foil, laying a pat of butter on top of the fish and scattering it with herbs and seasoning before you fold in the edges. Seal to make an airtight parcel and freeze. To serve, put the required number of parcels on a baking sheet in the frozen state and cook in a moderately hot oven (375°F, 190°C, Gas Mark 5) for 40 minutes. Poultry portions and small cuts of meat can be frozen and cooked the same way. For slimmers leave out the pat of butter.

To prevent oily fish from darkening, glaze it by first open freezing, then dip it in iced water until a thin coating of ice forms over it. Mould in foil, label and seal.

A variation of parcel cooking is to seal and freeze the food in a boilable bag. The bag of food can be heated in a pan of boiling water. Preparing the food and enclosing it in a bag to cook in its own juices makes good nutritional sense. There are two ways of sealing the food inside the bag so that it can be immersed in a pan of boiling water.
1. The first type of seal is that used with an open-ended bag and does not require a heat sealer. The closure can be of plastic-coated metal which is twisted around the top of the bag after expelling the excess air with the heel of the hand. Another method is to plunge the filled bag into a bowl of water to force out the excess air. These high density polythene bags should not be too tightly sealed – there must be sufficient space for the excess pressure to escape as the air in the bag heats up while the bag of food is bobbing about in the boiling water.
2. The second type is for use with a polythene bag, stronger still, which can be fully sealed

without allowing for a pressure build-up to burst the bag. Again, as much air as possible must be excluded and the bag must not be over-filled. This type of boilable bag comes with a special twine closure which shrinks when it becomes wet during reheating to make an even more effective seal.

I find these boilable bags particularly suitable for vegetables, cooked rice frozen with a pat of butter, sauces and portions of fish in a sauce.

Beetroot makes a good second vegetable served hot. Dice the cooked beetroot, mix with an equal quantity of apple purée. Add creamed horseradish and seasoning. Freeze in boiling bags (see above) and reheat in a pan of water with another vegetable.

Basic home-made ice cream is more exciting if it includes chopped nuts, crushed butterscotch sweets, chocolate chips, or ratafia biscuits to give an interesting variation in texture. Hazelnuts and chocolate make a good combination.

Buys of the month

Fish Mackerel, halibut, turbot, sole, sprats, Scottish salmon, prawns, shrimps, scallops, oysters
Meat, poultry and game Beef, pork, chicken, duck, duckling, goose, grouse, partridge, pheasant, plover, rabbit, venison, wild duck
Vegetables Aubergines, beetroot, Brussels sprouts, celery, leeks, marrows, onions, parsnips, peppers, potatoes, spinach, swedes, tomatoes, chestnuts
Fruit Apples, damsons, pears, nectarines, quinces, pumpkins, grapes

NOVEMBER

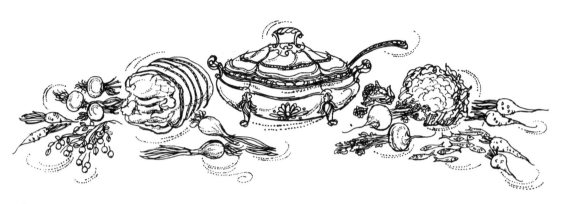

Chestnut soup

1 lb./450 g. chestnuts	1 oz./25 g. butter
1 onion	2 pints/generous litre
1 carrot	stock
1 potato	salt and pepper

Cut a cross in the chestnut shells and plunge them into boiling water for 10–15 minutes. Drain; when cool enough to handle, peel off the shell and brown under-skin. Roughly chop the onion, carrot and potato. Heat the butter in a large pan and use to sauté the vegetables for about 5 minutes. Add the chestnuts and stock and season well. Cover and simmer for about 30 minutes, or until the chestnuts are tender. Cool slightly, then liquidise or sieve the mixture and cool.

To freeze Pour into a polythene container, seal and label.

To serve Turn the frozen soup into a saucepan and heat very gently. Sprinkle with chopped parsley and add a dash of cream just before serving, if liked.

Cod with walnuts

1 medium onion	8 oz./225 g. small
1 clove garlic	tomatoes, skinned and
1 tablespoon olive oil	halved
1 oz./25 g. walnuts,	3–4 tablespoons dry
chopped	white wine
1 teaspoon grated lemon	4 portions cod, haddock
zest	or turbot, skinned
1 tablespoon lemon juice	salt and pepper

Chop the onion and crush the clove of garlic. Fry in the olive oil until soft. Stir in the chopped walnuts, lemon zest, lemon juice, tomatoes and white wine. Bring to simmering point, then add the fish portions. Simmer gently until tender. Arrange the cooked fish in a shaped foil dish. Season the sauce with salt and pepper to taste. Pour over the fish and leave to cool.

To freeze Cover with a lid or foil. Seal and label.

To serve Uncover and place, still frozen, in a moderately hot oven (375°F, 190°C, Gas Mark 5) for 30–40 minutes.

Fisherman's pie

12 oz./350 g. smoked haddock	4 oz./100 g. mushrooms
4 scallops	½ pint/3 dl. béchamel sauce
4 oz./100 g. soft roes	2 lb./1 kg. creamed potato
salt and pepper	

Cut the haddock into small pieces and put into a shaped foil container with the cleaned and chopped scallops and roes. Season well. Slice the mushrooms, add to the white sauce and simmer gently for 5 minutes. Pour this over the fish, then top with the potato, roughed-up with a fork. Bake in a hot oven (425°F, 220°C, Gas Mark 7) for about 30 minutes. Cool.

To freeze Cover with a lid or foil, seal and label.
To serve Defrost. Dot the potato with butter and reheat in a moderate oven (350°F, 180°C, Gas Mark 4) for about 35 minutes.

Polynesian pork

2 chicken stock cubes	1½ lb./¾ kg. cooked lean pork (from leg, or bladebone), diced
¾ pint/4 dl. boiling water	
3 bay leaves	
3 cloves	8 oz./225 g. fresh or frozen *ripe* pineapple, chopped
4 tablespoons corn oil	
1 large mild onion, chopped	
	1 tablespoon cornflour
4 large sticks celery, sliced	1–2 tablespoons curry powder
2 large carrots, grated	salt to taste

Dissolve the stock cubes in the boiling water. Add the bay leaves and cloves and allow to stand for at least 10 minutes. In a flameproof casserole, heat the oil and use to cook the onion, celery and carrot gently until limp but not coloured. Add the pork and pineapple and cook, stirring, for a further 2 minutes. Sprinkle in the cornflour and curry powder and stir over the heat for 3 minutes. Strain in the stock, bring to the boil, and simmer gently until smooth and slightly thickened, stirring continuously. Adjust the seasoning.

To freeze Divide the curry between two polythene containers, seal and label.
To serve Defrost, turn the contents into a saucepan and reheat gently to boiling point, stirring continuously. Serve with fluffy boiled rice. This recipe makes 6–8 servings.
Note The same recipe can be made with raw pork fillet. Slice very thinly and toss in the hot oil until pale golden brown before adding the vegetables.

Pheasant with grapes
(Illustrated overleaf)

4 oz./100 g. green grapes	1 young pheasant
1 tablespoon dry sherry	1 large slice fat bacon
1 tablespoon brandy (optional)	4 oz./100 g. crescent-shaped croûtons
1 oz./25 g. butter	1 bunch watercress

Peel the grapes and place in a small dish. Pour over the sherry and brandy (if used) and leave to stand.

Put the butter inside the prepared pheasant, cover the breast with the bacon. Place the pheasant in a roasting pan and cook in a moderately hot oven (400°F, 200°C, Gas Mark 6) for 30 minutes. Remove the bacon, baste the bird with the pan juices and strain over the liquid from the grapes. Return to the oven and cook for about a further 15 minutes, basting the bird frequently, until it is cooked. Transfer the pheasant to a warm serving dish. Reduce the juices in the roasting pan, by about half, by rapid boiling over a high heat. Strain over the pheasant and serve garnished with croûtons, grapes and watercress.

Salmis of game

(Illustrated overleaf)

2 oz./50 g. butter	4 oz./100 g. carrot,
1 guinea fowl or	chopped
partridge, or 2 pigeons	2 tablespoons brandy
salt and pepper	½ bottle dry red wine
2 oz./50 g. fat bacon	grated nutmeg
1 clove garlic	bouquet garni
1 tablespoon silverskin	1 oz./25 g. beurre manié
pickled onions	
4 oz./100 g. onion,	
chopped	

Melt the butter in a flameproof casserole and use to brown the game. Season with salt and pepper and cover. Cook over a low heat for 30 minutes. Remove from the heat and carve the game into serving portions. Keep hot.

Cut the carcase, winglets and giblets into pieces and place in a pan with ½ pint (3 dl.) water. Cover and simmer for 20 minutes. Cut the bacon into snippets and cook gently in the casserole together with the garlic, silverskin onions and chopped vegetables for 5 minutes. Increase the heat, pour over the warm brandy and ignite. Add the wine and sufficient strained giblet stock to cover the contents. Season with more salt and pepper; add the grated nutmeg and bouquet garni and cover and simmer for 45 minutes. Remove the bouquet garni. Add the beurre manié, in small pieces, whisking until the sauce is thick and smooth. Add the game portions. Cool.

To freeze Transfer to a large polythene container, or for short term storage freeze in the casserole. Seal and label.

To serve Defrost, reheat to boiling and simmer for 5 minutes. Store for a maximum of 2 months.

Tangerine-glazed chops

2 fresh tangerines	pinch ground ginger
2 tablespoons golden or	4 frozen loin or chump
corn syrup	lamb chops, defrosted
1 tablespoon soy sauce	

Squeeze the juice from the tangerines. Strain the juice and mix with the syrup, soy sauce and ground ginger. Place the lamb chops on the grill pan, brush with the tangerine glaze and grill for 8–10 minutes on one side. Turn the chops over, brush with glaze and grill for a further 5–8 minutes, until cooked through. Serve with hot rice.

Baked stuffed apples

4 cooking apples	1 oz./25 g. mixed dried
2 tablespoons dark soft	fruit
brown sugar	5 tablespoons water
1 teaspoon ground	
cinnamon	

Core the apples and score a horizontal line round the centre of each one. Place the apples in a shaped foil dish. Mix together the sugar and cinnamon and stuff the apples alternately with the dried fruit and sugar mixture, ending with sugar. Sprinkle the remaining sugar around the apples. Pour in the water and bake in a moderately hot oven (375°F, 190°C, Gas Mark 5) for 30–35 minutes. Cool.

To freeze Place the lid on the container. Seal and label.

To serve Defrost at room temperature for 1–2 hours. If required hot, place in a moderate oven (350°F, 180°C, Gas Mark 4) for 20–25 minutes. Serve with ice cream, cream or custard sauce.

Pheasant with grapes; salmis of game (see recipes on pages 54 and 55)

Orange crunch pudding

3 oz./75 g. cornflakes
3 eggs, separated
4 oz./100 g. castor sugar
2 tablespoons orange juice
1 tablespoon lemon juice
1 tablespoon grated orange zest
½ pint/3 dl. double cream

Crush the cornflakes and sprinkle a little in the bases of six individual foil containers. Beat the egg whites until they form peaks, then gradually beat in the sugar. In a small bowl, beat the egg yolks until thick, then stir in the fruit juices and grated zest. Lightly whip the cream and fold into the egg whites alternately with the egg yolk mixture. Spoon into the foil cases and sprinkle the remaining crushed cornflakes on top.
To freeze Cover with a lid or foil, seal and label.
To serve Defrost in the refrigerator for about 1 hour.

Chocolate spice cake

4 oz./100 g. margarine
7 oz./175 g. sugar
2 oz./50 g. plain chocolate
2 eggs, separated
¼ teaspoon salt
½ teaspoon mixed spices
½ teaspoon cinnamon
6 oz./175 g. self-raising flour
8 tablespoons milk
2 teaspoons finely chopped candied peel
Icing
1 oz./25 g. butter
3 teaspoons cocoa
5 oz./150 g. icing sugar
1 tablespoon boiling water
few drops vanilla essence

Cream together the margarine and sugar until light and fluffy. Melt the chocolate in a basin over hot water and blend into the creamed mixture with the egg yolks. Mix the salt and spices with the flour and fold this into the mixture alternately with the milk. Beat the egg whites until stiff and fold in with the candied peel. Pour into a well greased 8-inch (20-cm.) cake tin and bake in a moderate oven (325–350°F, 160–180°C, Gas Mark 3–4) for about 45 minutes. Cool.
To make the icing, cream the butter and beat in the cocoa and icing sugar. Gradually stir in the boiling water, and finally the vanilla essence, beating well. Spread this icing over the cake and allow to set.
To freeze Open freeze until solid then pack in foil or a polythene bag or container, seal and label.
To serve Unwrap, place on a serving plate and allow to defrost for 4 hours at room temperature.

Freezing hints

Game birds for freezing should be plucked, drawn and hung for one day less than usual as they will mature further during the defrosting period. Begin roasting the bird while it is still slightly chilled. Store for up to 8 months.

Hare is often too tough for roasting, apart from the saddle, which many people enjoy. To prepare a large one or two smaller hares, remove the saddle and keep it aside for roasting. Store uncooked for a maximum of 8 months. Defrost and roast as for meat. Jug the remaining cuts and store cooked for a maximum of 2 months.

Since thickened sauces sometimes separate in the freezer, a liaison of flour and butter (beurre manié) may be added at the reheating stage. To make a beurre manié, cream together butter and flour in the proportion of ½ oz. (15 g.) flour to ¾ oz. (20 g.) butter and whisk small pieces into a stew.

Buys of the month

Fish Mackerel, cod, halibut, haddock, whiting, sole, turbot, herring, sprats, scallops, oysters
Meat, poultry and game Pork, capon, chicken, goose, turkey, grouse, partridge, pheasant, plover, snipe, teal, hare, venison, guinea fowl, pigeon, wild duck
Vegetables Broccoli, Brussels sprouts, celery, leeks, onions, swedes, carrots, turnips, parsnips, chestnuts
Fruit Apples, pears, cranberries, mandarins, tangerines, satsumas

DECEMBER

Christmas pâté

½ oz./15 g. lard
6 oz./175 g. liver
1 onion, chopped
6 oz./175 g. cooked
   turkey or chicken
2 oz./50 g. bacon
4 oz./100 g. sausage meat

1 egg, beaten
1 teaspoon
   Worcestershire sauce
1 tablespoon lemon juice
salt and pepper
2 tablespoons red wine

Melt the lard in a frying pan and use to brown the liver and onion. Put them through a mincer, together with the turkey or chicken and the bacon. Add all other ingredients and a little water if necessary to give a smooth consistency. Place mixture in a loaf tin and bake, uncovered, in a moderate oven (350°F, 180°C, Gas Mark 4) for 1½ hours. Cool.

To freeze Cover with foil, or pack in a polythene bag. Seal and label.

To serve Defrost overnight in the refrigerator. Serve sliced with a selection of salad vegetables, or as a sandwich filling.

Turkey chestnut cream

1 lb./450 g. cooked
   turkey
1 medium onion
4 oz./100 g. cooked
   chestnuts
2 oz./50 g. butter
1 oz./25 g. flour

½ pint/3 dl. turkey or
   chicken stock
½ pint/3 dl. milk
salt and pepper
1 teaspoon dried mixed
   herbs

Finely dice the turkey and finely chop the onion and chestnuts. Melt the butter and use to sauté the onion and chestnuts. Stir in the flour, then gradually add the stock and milk, stirring well, until the mixture boils and is smooth and thickened. Season and add the herbs and diced meat. Cool.

To freeze Pour into a polythene container, seal and label.

To serve Turn, still frozen, into a saucepan and reheat through gently. Use to fill pancakes, vol-au-vents or omelettes, or serve on triangles of buttered toast as a supper dish.

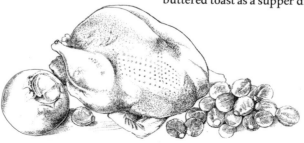

Walnut-lemon farce

2 sticks celery
2 oz./50 g. butter
6 oz./175 g. fresh white
   breadcrumbs
grated zest and juice of
   1 lemon
2 oz./50 g. walnuts, finely
   chopped
1 tablespoon dried sweet
   herbs
salt and pepper
1 egg
chicken stock

Finely chop the celery and fry in the butter until beginning to soften. Tip into a bowl and add the remaining ingredients, blending the mixture together with the lightly beaten egg and sufficient chicken stock to make a good firm stuffing consistency.
To freeze Pack in polythene bags. Seal and label. Store for a maximum of 4 weeks.
To use Defrost and use to stuff a defrosted turkey the day before roasting.

Iced Camembert

1 ripe Camembert cheese
1 demi-sel or 3 oz./75 g.
   cream cheese
2 tablespoons hot milk
3 tablespoons whipped
   cream
salt and freshly ground
   pepper
To serve
lemon wedges
paprika pepper

Cut the rind from the Camembert, taking care not to waste any of the cheese. Pound the cheese in a mortar, or rub through a sieve until quite smooth. Work the cream cheese with hot milk until smooth. Blend the cheeses together and add the cream. Season to taste with salt and pepper.
To freeze Pack the mixture into small plastic containers, coupes or dariole moulds. Seal and label.
To serve Either dip the mould into hot water and turn the cheese mixture out, or leave in mould. Dust lemon wedges with paprika and use to garnish the moulds. Serve with hot salted biscuits.

Délice de Noël

12 oz./350 g. chestnut
   purée
2 tablespoons lemon juice
2 tablespoons brandy
4 oz./100 g. icing sugar
½ pint/3 dl. double cream
4 egg whites

Sieve the chestnut purée. Beat in the lemon juice and brandy, then the sifted icing sugar. Half whip the cream and fold into the purée; fold in the stiffly beaten egg whites.
To freeze Spoon into individual serving dishes. Cover with foil, seal and label.
To serve Serve chilled, with tiny meringues or ginger biscuits. Store for a maximum of 3 months.

Fruity bakewell

6 oz./175 g. shortcrust
   pastry
2 oz./50 g. butter
4 oz./100 g. castor sugar
1 egg
1 large cooking apple
1½ oz./40 g. sultanas
finely grated zest and
   juice of 1 lemon

Roll out the pastry and use to line an 8-inch (20-cm.) foil flan case. Cream the butter and sugar together and add the beaten egg. Peel and coarsely grate the apple, mix with the sultanas, lemon juice and zest and add these to the creamed mixture. Pour into the pastry case and bake in a moderately hot oven (400°F, 200°C, Gas Mark 6) for 20 minutes, then reduce the heat to moderate (325°F, 160°C, Gas Mark 3) for a further 25 minutes, until the filling is set. Cool.
To freeze Cover with foil, seal and label.
To serve Place the frozen bakewell in a moderately hot oven (400°F, 200°C, Gas Mark 6) for about 20 minutes. Decorate with pieces of angelica and chopped glacé cherries. Serve hot or cold.

Traditional roast turkey garnished with cranberry sauce in scooped-out orange halves

Mincemeat splits

8 oz./225 g. self-raising	5 oz./150 g. lard
flour	about ¼ pint/1½ dl. water
½ teaspoon salt	mincemeat

Mix the flour and salt together in a basin. Cut the lard into small pieces and mix with the flour – using a knife – do not rub in. Add cold water and mix to a stiff paste. Turn on to a floured board and roll out to a narrow strip; fold this into three, turn one of the open ends towards you and roll out again. Repeat three times, always rolling away from you. Divide into two and roll out thinly to a square. Place one piece on a baking sheet and spread fairly thickly with mincemeat. Dampen the edges of the pastry all round and cover with the other pastry piece. Press the edges together well and trim neatly. Mark lines on the top lightly with a knife, from corner to corner, making a diamond pattern.

To freeze Open freeze until solid, remove from the sheet and pack in foil or a polythene bag. Seal and label.

To serve Unwrap, place on a greased baking sheet and brush over with beaten egg. Bake in a hot oven (425–450°F, 220–230°C, Gas Mark 7–8) for 30 minutes. Sprinkle the top with castor sugar and serve cut into squares.

Freezing hints

At least one week before Christmas, allocate a freezer basket or shelf to the items required for the great day. Remove them in the order required for defrosting, starting with the turkey – four days beforehand if it is a large one. Two days beforehand, transfer the stuffings to the refrigerator, so that they will be ready to stuff the bird with on Christmas Eve. On Christmas morning take out the mince pies, the vegetables, including the roast potatoes if these have been frozen, and the brandy or rum butter. Last of all, transfer a frozen pudding (see opposite) to the refrigerator just before the meal begins. Serve the turkey with the traditional accompaniments and with a garnish of cranberry sauce placed in scooped-out orange halves.

Some people find a traditional hot Christmas pudding too rich. Instead soften 2 pints (generous litre) of vanilla ice cream just sufficiently to fold in 4 oz. (100 g.) chopped mixed nuts, 4 oz. (100 g.) chopped mixed candied fruits and a miniature bottle of apricot brandy. Press the mixture into a 2-pint (1-litre) mould, seal or cover with foil and freeze. To serve, dip quickly into hot water, remove the seal and turn out the ice cream mould. Put a sprig of holly on top. Store for a maximum of 2 months.

Freeze the stuffing separately from the poultry as it may remain frozen and be uncooked even though the bird is cooked.

Do not forget that the carcase of the turkey can be made into excellent soup for freezing. Break up the carcase, add any leftover pieces of flesh, a selection of root vegetables and a couple of chicken stock cubes, with sufficient water to cover well. Simmer gently for about 2 hours. Cool, strain off carefully into polythene tumblers. If you have a minimum of 12 oz. (350 g.) of cooked turkey meat, it makes an excellent curry. If you prefer a sweet curry, stir in any leftover cranberry sauce. Store for a maximum of 2 months.

Buys of the month

Fish Mackerel, cod, halibut, haddock, whiting, sole, plaice, turbot, herring, sprats, scallops, oysters

Meat, poultry and game Pork, capon, chicken, duck, goose, turkey, grouse, partridge, pheasant, plover, snipe, teal, hare, venison, pigeon, wild duck

Vegetables Jerusalem artichokes, Brussels sprouts, celery, onions, parsnips, swedes, leeks, chestnuts

Fruit Apples, cranberries, pineapple, tangerines, mandarins, grapes

INDEX

Apple:
To freeze apples 7, 35
Baked stuffed apples 55
French apple flan 32
Apricot chiffon 32
Asparagus:
Cream of asparagus soup 28
Aubergine:
Spicy stuffed aubergines 50

Bean salad, dressed 40
Beef:
Beef and bean pot 17
Beefy pepperpots 34
Gingered kebabs 15
My beef stew 46
Steak and pigeon casserole 44
Beetroot 52
Beurre manié 57
Black cherry pudding 34
Blackberry crumble cake 46
Blanching vegetables 43
Butterscotch sauce 10

Cheese:
To freeze cheese 11
Cheesy fish cakes 10
Iced Camembert 59
Chestnut soup 53
Chicken:
Chain cooking 27
Chicken en cocotte 18
Chicken and mushroom pie 18
First blossom chicken 24
Chicory with ham 14
Chocolate spice cake 57
Christmas pâté 58
Cod with walnuts 53
Cottage cheese, banana and walnut
teabread 20
Country currant pies 38
Courgettes dorées 30
Crab in cream 34
Croûtons 31
Cucumber and herb flan 46
Curry-in-a-hurry 15

Délice de Nöel 59
Duck frozen in aspic jelly 27
Duck with orange and cherry sauce 24

Egg custards, to freeze 22
Eggs, to freeze 22
Eve's plum pudding 42

Fish *See also* Cod, Haddock, Salmon
Breton shells 38
Cheesy fish cakes 10

Fish in scallop shells 39
Parcel cooking of fish 52
Forcemeat balls 14
Fritters, fresh fruit 26
Frosted coupes 10
Fruit *See also* Apple, Apricot etc.
To prepare and freeze fruit 7, 35
Fresh berry jam 36
Fresh fruit fritters 26
Fruit salad for the freezer 47
Fruity bakewell 59
Fudge 51

Game, salmis of 55
Game soup 12
Ginger brownies 31
Gingerbread, spiced 51
Gingered kebabs 15
Golden grapefruit sponge 16
Golden raisin roll 10
Gooseberry party mousse 34
Green pea soup 36

Haddock:
Fisherman's pie 54
Haddock omelettes 30
Smoked haddock in onion milk 30
Ham, chicory with 14
Hare:
To prepare and store hare 57
Jugged hare with forcemeat balls 14
Herbs, to freeze 35

Ice cream Christmas pudding 61

Jaffa cheesecake 15
Jam, fresh berry 36
Jerusalem artichokes, to freeze 16

Lamb:
Curry-in-a-hurry 15
Lamb chop casserole 38
Lamb kebabs 24
Noisettes of lamb 28
Tangerine-glazed chops 55
Lemon curd 20
Lemon vichyssoise 8

Marinades 26, 27
Marrow and tomato scramble 42
Mincemeat splits 61
Mint sauce 31
Mocha walnut fudge 51

Nutty orange bread 19

Orange:
To freeze Seville oranges 11

Jaffa cheesecake 15
Nutty orange bread 19
Orange crunch pudding 57

Pancakes, to freeze 22
Pâté:
Christmas pâté 58
Pâté in aspic 42
Pigeon pâté 23
Peaches, to freeze 7, 39
Pear dumplings 47
Pheasant with grapes 54
Pigeon pâté 23
Pineapple castles 19
Pineapple and mint sorbet 30
Poacher's pasties 18
Pork:
Polynesian pork 54

Rabbit:
Poacher's pasties 18
Tipsy rabbit pudding 51
Rhubarb and orange cups 19
Rhubarb raisin crumble 26
Rhubarb tart 12

Salmon mousse 48
Scones 38
Shrimp bisque 40
Soups:
Chestnut soup 53
Cream of asparagus soup 28
Game soup 12
Green pea soup 36
Lemon vichyssoise 8
Shrimp bisque 40
Soupe au pistou 50
Spinach soup 23
Turkey soup 61
Spinach soup 23
Strawberries, to freeze 39

Tangerine-glazed chops 55
Tomato sauce, rich 44
Turkey and celery casserole 8
Turkey chestnut cream 58
Turkey soup 61

Vegetables *See also* Asparagus etc.
To blanch vegetables 43
To prepare and freeze vegetables 6
Vegetable curry sauce 17
Victoria sandwich, one-stage 20
Viennese hazelnut cake 43

Walnut-lemon farce 59
Wholewheat picnic scones 38